D0943269

iConscious
Accelerating Human Potential

Carole Griggs, PhD and Ted Strauss

Dedication

This book is dedicated to rapid whole-being awakening for all humans.

Acknowledgements

To us, this book is one piece in our larger endeavor to accelerate human development through modeling, assessment tools, writings, web offerings, coaching and leadership programs, consulting, and AI applications, all of which have helped shape this book. In that light, we want to acknowledge and honor...

- Susanne Cook-Greuter for encouraging us to bring forth our model and support us as an advisor.
- Dawa Tarchin Phillips for his unerring wise advice on leadership, conscious entrepreneurship, conscious marketing, and strategic directions.
- Mikey Siegal for supporting our efforts from the start of our work.
- Karen Jaenke for welcoming us to teach our framework at John F Kennedy University.
- Jonathan Robinson for his humor, comradery and cheerful support.
- Jakob Possert for his many dedicated hours, employing his scholarly rigor to help us refine our model and compare it with others, develop the iConscious Assessment, and edit this book.
- Ava St. Claire for her work translating our perspective into a beautiful website.
- Ted for spending countless hours editing, finding images and quotes, and preparing the text and cover for publishing.

iConscious Reviews

"Griggs' and Strauss's new book offers a richly textured, systemic model of human consciousness development. It consists of 5 domains that need to be addressed to fulfill human integration. I particularly appreciate their emphasis on the domain of Uniqueness in each person's development process; I've not seen that anywhere else. The authors offer detailed descriptions of the whole system as well as the 14 stages and 5 domains of growth. Especially valuable for readers are quotes, examples and helpful practices that progressively deepen the experience of various states and stages for those interested in practice. The book is written as a plea for accelerating development in the hope to find mature solutions to our current global distress."

– Dr. Susanne R. Cook-Greuter, independent scholar, coach and consultant

"The iConscious model is truly groundbreaking, bridging the gap between human development and the evolution of consciousness, and deepening our understanding of how people grow. Carole and Ted integrate dozens of models with their experience of coaching thousands of clients to accelerate what they call conscious human development. If you're a coach or leader, or passionate about your own self-development, I highly recommend this leading-thought book."

– Karen Jaenke, PhD, Chair, Consciousness & Transformative Studies, JFK University

"Carole and Ted are pioneers in developing a deep and integrated model of awakening that will help humanity move into its next phase of development."

– Mikey Segal, founder of Consciousness Hacking

Contents

Section 1:
Introduction

Are you ready to awaken your consciousness, maximize your potential, and fulfill your unique purpose? Are you drawn to help others do the same? This book offers a new way to accelerate personal transformation far beyond what most are aware is possible.

Imagine you're lost in a foreign city and you have no map or GPS. You can ask the locals which places are best to see and how to get there, but you'll get as many opinions as people you ask. You could spend weeks wandering around, feeling like you're wasting your time. Now imagine you have a GPS, you have clear destination to visit, and clear directions to each. Instead of taking weeks to do very little, you will accomplish a lot in a matter of days.

Like that, the iConscious™ framework offers a map that accelerates human development by showing you where you are, where you're going, and how to get there most directly. It makes clear where the detours are and how to develop in an integrated way, maximizing hh success for you and those around you. If you are a coach, leader, HR director, educator, mentor, consultant, therapist, parent, or supporter of anyone, this framework will help you and those you coach thrive.

Challenges

In our decades of coaching work, we've seen the same set of problems and challenges appear repeatedly, with negative impacts on all levels of human life. Here are just a few of them:

1- Individual

It's clear to us that everyone goes through a process of evolution that can ultimately bring fulfillment to their unique life purpose, both personally and professionally. But it's also clear that most people don't get the chance to unfold their gifts and potentials nearly as deeply as is possible. In our experience, a major reason for this is a lack of clear understanding about how humans grow in an integrated way. This leads to a lack of clear direction for our most positive evolution. It also leads to partial development in some areas, and a lack of development in others.

Without an understandable model of development or method for assessing progress, most people – including those who've spent decades in numerous personal development programs – have little to no idea where they are in their process or where they are going. We often see people getting overwhelmed or distracted by the multitude of trendy options available for personal growth that don't honor individual uniqueness or current developmental stages. This results in confusion, slow growth, and a lot of time and money wasted on ineffective personal development efforts. It also causes a lot of unnecessary suffering, lack of fulfillment and ongoing difficulties in both business and personal life. These difficulties are extremely costly not just in time and money, but also in energy, wellness, and lost opportunities.

One day at a personal growth conference, a woman came up to us, saying "Every year, I spend thousands of dollars on meditation and personal development workshops, but I don't seem to be making much progress. I'm just as anxious and confused as I was ten years ago. I feel like I'm throwing darts blindfolded, hoping I'll hit a bulls' eye I can't see. There must be a better way."

This describes a tragedy we see playing out in millions, if not billions of human beings. We find that people are most healthy and productive when they're developing consistently. But when growth is slow, we live with the pain of knowing we're not using our full potential, and feeling stuck, missing the point, or wasting our lives. This brings ever-deepening existential pain. Not knowing how to deal with this pain often results in bad decisions, such as abusing ourselves with food, drugs, alcohol, workaholism, or fighting with co-workers or loved ones, all in an attempt to escape discomfort. All such reactions result in degrading the quality of our life. It makes us so sad when we see people who've spent decades, tied up in knots, avoiding themselves, unaware of their true potentials, and hopeless about ever finding a better way.

2- Coaches and Leaders

Coaches and leaders often lack a practical, whole-being way to assess where a client or employee's gaps and growing edges are, making the job unnecessarily challenging. Without a framework for understanding the development process and what guidance is appropriate at each stage, it's hard to know how to help people in a direction that brings real evolutionary change, versus just teaching skills or helping with choices.

Leaders and mentors are often attracted to models that can help point the way to deeper development. Yet we've noticed that most models tend to be too simple (often just one dimensional, conflating domains and confusing the process), too complex (therefore hard to understand or apply), or not high enough resolution (conflating stages and reducing coaching effectiveness). Also, most models don't clearly show how we can grow in a way that helps to integrate the main facets of who we are, which contributes to split (and therefore slow) overall development.

3- Businesses and Organizations

To maintain their competitive edge, companies need their employees to be fully engaged using their deepest capacities. Nonprofit organizations, educational institutions and government entities need the same focused commitment from workers in order to serve their customers effectively. But when employees don't know who they are, what their purpose is, or what matters to them, they're not very inspired or engaged, and they can't bring their best. They also can't give their best if they are operating from a place of self-negation, if they feel that something is wrong with them, or if they are seeing the world through fractured or polarized perspectives. Nor can they thrive if they can't communicate or collaborate well, or if they avoid discomfort or conflict. And giving them new tools and techniques doesn't get to the root of these problems.

The root of such problems is that people are often unaware of who they are, why they're here (in life), and how to feel settled in their own skin. The result is that many spend their lives resisting their job. Others, desperate to be seen or loved, are unaware of the sources of their inner pain, how magnificent they truly are, or why they uniquely matter. This results in an incalculable waste of money and human resources, and an endless migration of workers from one company to the next as employees search for themselves and their purpose. It also contributes to the creation of products and services that end up causing at least as much harm as good, negatively affecting the company, its employees, humanity, and the environment.

Businesses are always looking for cutting edge approaches to improve their success. But if success is defined only in monetary terms for the business owners, the results are often disappointing for everyone involved. The next great breakthrough is unlikely to come from a better method for selling widgets. We believe it will come from people who tap into their full potential as human beings. When human beings work together to bring out the best in each other, that becomes the new standard for success.

The challenge for organizations isn't simply about how to actualize individual and team potentials. It's also about knowing how to hire the right people. When hiring is done solely on the basis of education, experience, and skills, crucial pieces are missing, including personal development, alignment with purpose, stage of consciousness, and relational capacities. Without taking such factors into consideration, it's impossible to achieve high productivity and flow.

4- Humanity

Humanity is facing a growing number of existential threats including climate change, depleted natural resources, collapse of ecosystems, and the rise of dangerous artificial intelligence often motivated by greed. Each of these problems is enormous, but taken together it's clear that for humanity to survive with any hope of thriving, we must quickly become conscous, wiser, more caring, and more aware of our impact on each other, our work, and our environment. We cannot continue doing business as usual from the same limited stages of development that got us into these dire circumstances because we can no longer afford it. The cost of living in unawareness of our deep connectedness with life is being revealed through tragedies already playing out on a global scale.

We see the above problems for individuals, coaches, leaders, organizations, and humanity as human development challenges. From our perspective, these problems are solvable when clearly understood from a larger, integrative perspective.

Solutions

"Problems cannot be solved from the same level of consciousness that created them." –Albert Einstein

As Einstein put it, if we're to solve such enormous problems, we must change our level of consciousness. It's no longer enough to simply learn some new skills and how to apply them. It's not enough to transcend ourselves and know that our consciousness exists beyond our personal lives. And it's also not enough to just have an extremely high IQ and not know how to deeply feel, relate, or communicate. We must each evolve our *whole being* to know our unity with all humans and all of life. *When we know unity, we are unable to continue harming those around us without noticing we are harming ourselves*. When we directly experience that others are part of our very self, our relationship with ourselves, others, and life begins to self-correct. We become spontaneously loving toward ourselves and others, we're more creative, and we create wiser, more sustainable solutions to our individual and collective problems.

There's a wealth of scientific evidence that shows higher stages of development increases feelings of love and compassion for self and others[1], increases happiness and well-being[2], gives more continuous access to flow states[3], improves physical and mental health[4], reduces mortality rates[5], improves outcomes as team players and collaborators[6], increases productivity and wealth[7], improves living standards[8], increases available choices[9], boosts fulfillment of purpose and potential[10], improves quality of life[11], brings more fulfillment to relationships[12], and increases concern for other species and the environment[13]. To us, it is clearly evident that accelerating human development is a fundamental key to solving our individual and collective problems.

What's the rush?

When we speak of accelerating human development, we often hear people wonder if we're forcing a process that needs to take its natural time. What's the rush?

To us, it's not about rushing; it's about removing the obstacles to growth by nourishing our existential roots. Imagine a large city of very small bamboo plants living in the desert. Given the lack of water, it's easy to picture why the inhabitants of this city would assume it's normal for growth to be slow. Now imagine a village of bamboo plants in a jungle not far away, with plenty of water and nutrients to support their growth. They're growing 85 feet in 30 days! To the bamboo plants struggling in the desert, news of such super-plants might stimulate responses like "that's impossible," or "that seems unnaturally fast". Some plants will even think "those must be incredibly special and unusual plants to be able to grow like that." But to the thousands of bamboo plants thriving in the jungle, growing rapidly feels incredibly natural. It also feels a lot better than living in the desert, always feeling hungry and thirsty, fighting over every last drop of nourishment.

It's our observation that human beings today grow at a lifetime average rate of about one stage every 20 years.

This looks very slow to us, and appears mostly due to a lack of understanding about who we are as human beings and how we can nourish our evolution. In our experience, when adults get support for integrative evolution with appropriate guidance, they tend to grow about 10-20 times faster than average.

From our perspective, this is neither impossibly nor unnaturally fast. In fact, it feels far more natural to evolve quickly, use our deeper potentials, and fulfill our purpose. It appears to us that the rate of human evolution is accelerating almost daily as we continue learning more about how human beings evolve.

Is rapid evolution better? From our perspective the answer is an unequivocal YES, both from our personal experience with thousands of clients and from the wealth of scientific research that goes far beyond the few studies we referenced above. Accelerating human evolution is better for individuals, groups, businesses, nations, the environment, and the world.

Why is it so important to stimulate human growth? Because everything we do is limited by our capacity, which in turn is based on our level of development. When we are not well developed, we cannot process complexity well, our perspective is narrower, and we tend to make short-sighted decisions that are not in our best interests.

It's not that we don't get anything done when we are less developed, but the world we create from that space is far less than ideal, and rapidly becoming more dangerous than we can afford. Many of our technologies are actively harming us, whereas everything we create could actively help us, if only we were aware and developed enough to notice that everything we do and create impacts not only ourselves, but everyone around us and all of life. Accelerating human development brings us to stages in which we are liberated enough to care about each other and respond to challenges with the love, respect, subtlety and complexity our current world demands.

What's possible?

We find that people don't know their own potential until they learn about it and are loved and supported in directions that help them personally evolve. When these pieces are in place, previously unattainable things suddenly become possible.

On the individual level, every human being can deeply awaken their gifts, realize their unity with life, heal their deepest wounds, be passionately creative, and fulfill their unique purpose. But perhaps even more important, everyone can evolve from living in resistance to self and life, to accepting and embracing what is, to living in deep flow. Each of us has the capacity to live in such surrender to life's unpredictable ups and downs that most of our energies are liberated to serve others.

Relationally, we can grow to respect each other deeply, co-create with passion, and find intimacy that fills our hearts with gratitude. Collectively, we can embrace our differences, cooperate in solving our global problems, and expand the horizons of humanity's potential.

It's important to underscore that these are not just theories or idealistic goals; these are living realities we help people grow into every day. You may be thinking "That sounds great, but how could that possibly be achieved?" In our experience, coaching people into living their higher potential is actually far easier than bringing them up to current average levels. Once people have met their basic needs, evolution to higher stages only requires the five keys to acceleration we'll describe below.

How can we accelerate human development?

To accelerate human development, we must understand the primary dimensions of our life and how we evolve in each of them. Within the iConscious framework, we offer a research-based model of human evolution that addresses what we have found to be the 3 most important dimensions: 1) the 5 Domains of our being, 2) the 4 Views we look through, and 3) the 14 Stages of development through which we evolve.

The 5 Domains are Consciousness, Uniqueness, Mind, Emotions, and Body. The 4 Views are Subjective (our personal internal experience), Observable (what can be perceived and measured externally), Relational (shared internal experiences in relationship with others), and Systemic (how we fit into the larger external systems we are part of). We divide Development into 3 Phases (Dual, Unified, and Singular), each of which contains a number of Stages that represent important steps in our growth.

In this book, we describe each of these three dimensions in greater detail, along with the needs and best practices in each Domain at each Stage. We also include images, quotes, and examples at each of these "Locations". On our website we also offer the iConscious Assessment, an instrument for determining one's personal evolutionary stage in a range of development that's much larger than what most are aware is possible. It's our experience that when you understand where you are and how to evolve to the next level, evolution accelerates for you and often for those around you.

While there is plenty of individual uniqueness in the awakening process, the iConscious model is designed to show *on average* what the process is and where it's taking you. This understanding helps you find where you are and get appropriate guidance to grow directly. If you are coaching, leading, hiring, or supporting others, you can use the information in this book and in our Coaches and Leaders Program to locate a person's development and offer guidance that will be maximally effective. In our experience, this is absolutely key to accelerating the personal evolution process and preventing unnecessary dead ends and detours along the way. When you understand this framework for yourself, you'll be able to use it to help yourself and those around you to grow and thrive as never before.

Keys to acceleration

Below are five primary factors we have found to be most important in accelerating human development:

1- Sufficient resources

To grow, we must first survive. While people are in survival mode, development is a lower priority. Once we have food, water, a stable place to live, reasonably good physical and mental health, and some free time, we can investigate ourselves and our world. It's of primary importance that we learn to take care of our basic needs, including survival, health, and finances so we can afford to take time to find ourselves and fulfill our unique purpose.

2- The drive to explore

As soon as we no longer need to use all our energy and attention to survive and fulfill basic needs, it's natural for humans to explore. We are curious; we want to know who we are, what life is about, why we exist, and how we fit in. But it's important to know that we can find our own answers to our big questions. If, due to conditioning or past disappointments, you believe you can't actually find what you're searching for, you may become hopeless or uninspired, moving through life without a real connection with your own passion. You might even lose track of why life matters or why *you* matter. But if you can connect with your drive to explore and believe you can find what you seek, nothing can stop you.

In 1961, John F. Kennedy inspired the human drive to explore outer space. That drive was there waiting to be tapped, but Kennedy's famous speech provided a vision of what we could accomplish, and the results were almost miraculous. Our vision is to make it easy for all people to explore both inner and outer space, discover our own deeper potentials, and bring positive transformation to humanity and our planet.

3- Integration

By understanding the three dimensions of the iConscious framework (Domains, Views, and Development), we become aware of aspects of our own being we must explore in order to know ourselves. But without understanding the importance of integration, it's easy to get lost in the details of any of these facets. If we get lost in any one dimension, we can lose track of what it means to develop in a holistic way.

In our experience, taking an integrative perspective causes personal development to accelerate far faster than not doing so. We find that the vast majority of adults are well developed in one or two Domains, and quite underdeveloped in the others. This results in what we call the "bungee effect". While we strive to grow in one or more Domains that we value (and are usually good at), we are being unconsciously held back by our lack of development (or trauma) in other Domains that we don't see, don't value, or are afraid to encounter. For example, if we value mind, but believe that emotions are unimportant, then our feelings will keep trying to break out of their box and get our attention (usually at the most inappropriate moments) because they are, in fact, part of who we are, whether we are ready to own them or not.

The iConscious model shows the evolutionary trajectories of all 5 Domains together. This makes it easy to understand how some people can be extremely advanced in one or more Domains, yet less developed in others, resulting in uneven development. The model makes it clear that today such splits or imbalances are far more common than integrated development. In our experience, such lack of integration between the Domains causes huge delays in personal growth, and tremendous waste of human and material resources.

To understand this, picture someone you know who is a genius at something (such as a technical wizard), yet who is challenged in the art of relating with others, particularly when it comes to conflict or difficult relational situations. Or someone who is great at business yet is feared by those around them. Unintegrated, even sociopathic personalities seem normal simply because our western world is filled with them. Part of our mission is to help heal and integrate such splits by making it clear what integration can look like and how we can get there most directly.

In our view, healthy development integrates all 5 of the Domains we mentioned as well as all 4 Views. When we are encouraged to work with all Domains and Views, we evolve far more quickly and experience forms of wellness, fulfillment, and depth of potential that were previously unknown or inaccessible.

Another way to say this is that taking a holistic view on human development results in holistic maturity, which turns out to be a far more effective and enjoyable way to live, vs. simply accumulating knowledge and skills but never fully healing ourselves or realizing our deeper potentials. People who are developed in a well-rounded way are deeply engaged with their work, have patience and compassion for themselves and others, experience healthy personal and work relationships, profound fundamental wellness, and unstoppable personal purpose.

4- Appropriate guidance

What we mean by appropriate guidance is support from one or more skilled coaches, leaders, or counselors who understand how we grow and what's most helpful at each stage. If those supporting us get impatient with where we are in our development, we feel judged, misunderstood, and unsupported. If our leaders think we're at a less or more evolved stage than where we actually are, we will not feel met, and our growth will be hindered.

Have you ever experienced the joy and benefit of working with a really great mentor or coach? We have both experienced the benefits of being supported by those who have walked the path before us, making our own progress tremendously easier. Having a great guide and a clear development model can lead to remarkable results.

When coaching also takes into consideration which Domains need the most help, development can be integrated because we're not leaving any important part of ourselves behind. You can imagine if, for example, the entire focus in coaching was on how we develop psychologically, then our growth in consciousness, uniqueness, and body would suffer.

The same is true of the four Views. If we spend all our time in our own subjective (internal) experience, we are not truly sharing our lives with others, and we will suffer from the lack of nourishment we all need from others and community.

If we are not open to how others see us, we will be stuck in narcissism. And if we are unaware of the larger systems we're part of, we will be out of sync with the life we are intimately part of.

We also find that when guidance comes from a desire to help each person fulfill their personal needs, people evolve directly. When people are pushed to get over themselves or to experience things they don't sense they need, development will be slowed.

5- Openness to mystery

In our experience, appropriate guidance must honor the mystery of each person's absolute uniqueness. If we treat everyone as if they are the same, they will not feel deeply met or seen with their unique ancestry, their unique personal history, and their unique human gifts and limits. We have often noticed that when people are lovingly met and supported in the mystery of their uniqueness, they quickly open and blossom.

But openness to mystery also includes our capacity to welcome what we don't yet see and can't yet understand about life. Life throws us all kinds of confounding challenges, often leaving us wondering how we can understand and control what we don't like. We find it's important to understand that no matter how hard we try, we will have limited understanding or control at best. The more we can simultaneously embrace the uncontrollable mystery of life along with the challenges we *can* control, the more quickly we grow and step into fulfilling our purpose.

Our mission and vision

As co- founders of this work, it has been our lifelong passion to discover for ourselves and communicate to as many as possible the essences of what makes us human and how we can grow to live our deepest potential. In 2014, we were inspired to combine our extensive experience with cutting edge research to create a model anyone can use to help accelerate human thriving through coaching, personal development, interactive media, and artificial intelligence applications. We knew that having a clear roadmap would make it possible to assess an individual's current stage of development from multiple perspectives and give appropriate support to accelerate anyone's evolution towards a more fulfilled and happy life.

Our mission is to accelerate conscious human development both individually and collectively by working with individuals, coaches, leaders, and change-makers to bring this perspective into human culture. Our vision is to help create a world in which it is normal for human beings to awaken in all areas of life, give their deepest gifts, and create together in deeply attuned, collective consciousness.

Research

It was important for us to align our model with current research to bridge the gaps between academics, systems for personal and leadership development, and students and teachers of consciousness and nonduality. On our website (https://iconscious.global/research-charts/), we have charts showing how we organize the works of 27 respected human development researchers (including Piaget, Maslow,

Kohlberg, Beck and Cowen, Goleman, Mayer-Salovey, Kegan, Loevinger, and others) according to our framework. In the Apprendix, we've included our paper titled *Accelerating Conscious Human Development Using the iConscious Model as an Integrative Framework*.

As we began to align the first seven stages in the system with Ego Development, Spiral Dynamics, Integral Theory, and dozens of other systems, we noticed a large gap in the scientific awareness of the more developed stages. The iConscious Model expands upon the knowledge of the more evolved levels of human development by adding stages beyond those conventionally known, each broken into Domains with clear descriptions, needs, examples, and appropriate practices.

The first 7 stages in our model are based in the work of many researchers in the field. The stages beyond that are based on our coaching experience with thousands of clients as well as writings from many wisdom lineages describing experiences beyond our Stage 7. Also, our descriptions of domains within each stage are our own formulations of development based on our experience and available literature.

Hitting a nerve

As we clarified the descriptions in our model, we started talking more with leaders in the human development and consciousness evolution fields. We had no idea how our model would be seen by academics or teachers of consciousness. We got a lot of appreciation for our work, along with wonderfully helpful feedback. When we showed our model to the head of the department of consciousness and transformative studies at JFK university, we were immediately invited to create a course for their Masters program, exploring the history of personal development studies as seen through our model, which continues today.

We were then invited to speak at various conferences around the world, where we delivered our messages about humanity's need for clear, evidence-based support to realize our highest potentials (please see https://iconscious.global/media/ for recordings of our talks). We knew we really hit a nerve when we were invited to participate in the Loving AI project, using our model as a developmental framework for coaching dialogs between test subjects and the famous robot Sophia.

If a picture is worth a thousand words, a good video can be worth a million. On our media page, there's a video of Sophia using our model to guide interactions with various people seeking support for their personal development. Many people who view this video are amazed at how skillful and human-like the robot can be, and how big the impact can be on those being coached this way. We believe that robots and artificial agents can offer remarkably precise and effective guidance while being sensitive, more knowledgeable than any individual person, and available 24/7 to millions of people. The Loving AI experiments demonstrated that such dialogs increased feelings of self-love and love for others with strong statistical significance. For more on that project, please visit Loving AI.org.

The most gratifying result of our work so far has been its remarkable effectiveness. Our clients are growing rapidly and feeling much more fulfilled in their work and relationships, and the companies we consult with are growing by leaps and bounds. Recently, a woman who participated in one of our workshops found herself in tears, grateful to finally be able to see and understand her own development in the bigger picture. A large software company rounded a corner and accelerated into huge growth as soon as we brought our perspectives to the company's executives. This is the kind of transformation we live to empower.

We continue providing coaching to business leaders and individuals around the world, and we're also offering iConscious coaching certification courses. We have a passion to support leaders and coaches who want to help people grow in integrated ways to achieve deep engagement and the capacity to build innovative products and services that transform the world in positive ways.

Strengths and limits of models

Before introducing our model, we want to say a few things about the challenges and benefits of models in general. You may have heard the phrase "The map is not the territory." This phrase was coined by Alfred Korzybski in 1912 to highlight the gaps between the objective world and our mental ways of modeling it. We agree; no model can describe the infinitely unique ways in which each person goes through their own process of development. The mystery of who we are and how we grow cannot be fully defined, categorized, or confined by words, symbols, or models. The iConscious model is designed to describe the *average* experience so you can get a clearer sense of your own unique path.

Following are some common concerns we've heard about models, along with how we hold them:

- **Because they are reductive, models are partial.** Because this is true, developers must choose what elements to focus on. Some models represent cognitive or psychological development; others represent growth in consciousness, emotions, or body. Some focus on the subjective experience, others on what can be observed externally. Some focus only on the relational, cultural, or ecological views. Some models are presented as if they represent a holistic perspective, yet conflate important dimensions into a one-dimensional model of growth. We agree that there are a limited number of dimensions that can be modeled at once and still be understood, which is why we find that Stages, Domains, and Views works so well. Using these three important dimensions illuminates what integrated development looks like.

- **Models impose lines and boxes on what is actually a continuous spectrum of development.** This is true, and we find it useful to hold that seamless spectrum while simultaneously using lines and boxes to discriminate Stages and Domains to locate and accelerate development. We took the average descriptions of different stages of development and overlaid a grid. Although the grid lines appear to divide the Stages and Domains, in reality there are no such boundaries. We believe we've made our model in high enough resolution that anyone can not only understand the steps along the way, but can also step back and see the organic smoothness of the process.

- **Models can make the development process appear linear.** The process we call conscious human development is incredibly fluid and fuzzy, and the way that people grow is very organic and unique to each individual. The development process often appears to move us forward and backward as we oscillate toward deeper integration and unfoldment. Our growing edges can span several Stages. And yet, in our experience, the process is linear in the sense that, on average, people grow and expand toward deeper embodiment of their unique full potential when given loving, clear, and developmentally appropriate support and understandings.

- **An averaged model can't account for personal uniqueness or cultural influences.** We agree. Everyone has their unique ways of moving through the lifelong process of developing, and those ways are highly influenced by the cultures they grow in. Every culture has its own perspectives on human development and every individual has her or his own natural way of evolving. Despite huge differences in character and culture, the iConscious model uses what we find to be common markers to describe development. By including an understanding of the non-linearity of development (especially after Stage 6 in our model), we sense that our model can embrace cultures beyond those of modern western societies.

Now let's consider some of the strengths of models. By understanding the strengths, we can see the importance of using models to help us develop more directly.

- **Well-designed models are like GPS maps; they give perspective of the territory.** Once you can see the big picture of personal development, it's easier to understand where you are and how you relate to the larger process. Getting a broader view supports your capacity to lean into evolving different Domains without getting lost in the details. It also shows you where you are going, which helps you avoid pitfalls and detours along the way.

- **Models can simplify.** The process of developing toward our full potential can feel complex. But we need not be overwhelmed by that. The iConscious model can help you understand in simple terms how to maximize your evolution.

- **Models can reveal what we're not seeing.** When the periodic table of elements was created, it suddenly gave us a vision of what's going on in the subatomic world, prompting questions like, 'What if we add another proton over here?' This allowed us to discover all kinds of new elements that we could not previously see because we didn't have a model to help us understand what we were missing. The iConscious model is like that; it gives a big picture of the process, enabling us to better understand our personal and collective journey.

- **Models can organize knowledge.** Think about all the different books, seminars, and teachings that exist to help people evolve. When seen without an organizing principle, it appears impossible to understand how all those bits of information relate to each other, and how they relate to you. Once you understand the iConscious model, every piece of information about human development can be seen in an inclusive context, making it far easier to understand and apply in practical ways.

All models are limited because they can never fully represent the infinite mystery of human life. The strength of the iConscious model is its ability to help you understand where you are in your evolution, what areas you've not yet seen, and what the bigger picture looks like. This helps you understand where your process is taking you, what limitations you may encounter coming up, and how to deeply awaken your potential most directly with the least suffering and the fewest detours.

Please Note

Please be aware that we're not making value judgments about people who are more developed versus less developed. All human beings have existentially equal value because we are all part of life. But we find it's important to distinguish where people are in their process, so we can help them expand their capacity if that's what they desire.

Also, by offering this model, it doesn't mean we encourage you to think out your whole life through this framework. We're not trying to get you stuck in your head – actually, quite the opposite. This framework is designed to help free you from fixating in your mind (or in any one Domain or View) so you can find your most optimal direction.

Section 2:
The iConscious Model

The following pages show the iConscious model in four parts. It shows how we evolve in two important dimensions: Development and Domains. While our framework also includes the dimension of Views, we have not shown that in this particular version of the model because that would make it too visually complex, so we'll discuss Views in its own section below, and also in each Stage Summary in Sections 3-5. Please note that this version of the model shows all statements in Subjective View. To see all statements in the other 3 Views, please visit the interactive model on our website at iConscious.global.

The model describes development as it proceeds from left to right, which we've divided into 15 Stages grouped into three Phases (Dual, Unified, Singular). You'll notice that directly below each Stage number and its title is a box with a statement describing the overall features of that stage without regard to Domain. The features of each Domain within that Stage are listed below that.

Domains are displayed on the left side, stacked vertically.

These are the five important areas of our life that we encounter every day: Consciousness, Uniqueness, Mind, Emotions, and Body. They are arranged in approximate order of subtlety from unmanifest awareness at the top to concretely manifest physicality at the bottom.

As you look at the model, you'll see there are 70 boxes below the Stage headers and to the right of the Domains. We call these Locations. Each Location contains human potentials that can be realized and embodied. The statements in each Location describe the main features of development in that zone from the Subjective View.

We recommend reading all statements in the model as it will give you a direct understanding of the entire process. You may find it confusing to read beyond what you can relate to, but we find it helps induce deeper awakening when we have a basic understanding of where we're going and what's possible.

Following the model is a more detailed explanation of Development, Domains, and Views.

	Dual			
	1 Survival	**2** Self-Centric	**3** Conforming	**4** Rational Striving
	Primary focus on staying alive	Impulsive and self-absorbed	Conforming to identity group	Drive to know, prove, succeed, achieve, or win
Consciousness	Attention focused on immediate needs	Awareness absorbed in one's own immediate wants	Awareness developing within the limits of identity group	Controlling awareness to achieve wants
Uniqueness	Uniqueness expressed unconsciously	Limited awareness of the value of my uniqueness	Recognizing uniqueness acceptable to identity group	Using uniqueness to achieve wants
Mind	Thinking occupied with survival needs	Absorption in one's own thoughts	Only allowing thoughts & beliefs acceptable to identity group	Trying to rationally optimize one's life
Emotions	Survival-based instinctive emotional reactions	Emotionally self-absorbed	Only allowing feelings acceptable to identity group	Minimizing emotions to avoid complexity and achieve goals
Body	Instictive survival-based physical reactions	Exclusive focus on satisfying physical wants	Physical development shaped by social norms	Ignoring or over-managing one's body

© 2019 Whole Being Awakening

		Dual			
		5 Equality Harmony	**6** Inclusive	**7** Awakening	**8** Oscillating
		Promoting "oneness" by battling hierarchical differences	Identities crumble, creating flexibility, depth, and capacity for integration	Fundamental shifts and openings into boundlessness	Leaning into the discomfort of apparent opposites
Consciousness		Seeking universal connection, learning to witness experience	Expanding awareness starts dissolving limited sense of self	Awareness awakens as itself	Trying to hold the tension of being both finite and infinite
Uniqueness		Valuing uniqueness to promote egalitarian ideals	Starting to accept who one is and is not	Realizing and appreciation one's uniqueness	Identity alternates between personality and universal Being
Mind		Seeking peace of mind through positive thinking	Making sense of conflicting concepts	Able to witness thoughts from identity with spaciousness	Trying to hold the paradox of known and unknown
Emotions		Prioritizing love and positivity over disharmony	Learning to stay present with all emotions	Universal love is the space for all emotions	Trying to hold the tension of unconditional love and personal emotions
Body		Seeking harmony through physical disciplines	Noticing unaligned physical conditioning	Experiencing spaciousness in the body	Trying to hold awareness of body and spaciousness simultaneously

© 2019 Whole Being Awakening

	Unified			
	9 Embodied Unity	**10** Transforming	**11** Individuating	**12** Living Potential
	Nonseparate realization brings wholeness, wellness, and presence	Core duality-based conditioning surfaces for healing	Fundamentally untangled and liberated into life	Serving from alignment of purpose and power
Consciousness	Consciousness is experienced as unified with personal domains	Awareness illuminates and transforms deep wounds and conditioning	Deeply embodied presence in most situations	Serving from fully engaged presence
Uniqueness	Personality is realized as a non-separate expression of being	Fundamental healing of self negation	Liberated to live one's unique truth	Serving by living deepest purpose
Mind	Thoughts are known as aspects of being	Releasing self-deceiving beliefs	Liberated from internal chatter to think clearly and authentically	Serving from potent clarity
Emotions	Feeling emotions as waves of being	Unified awareness enables core healing of emotional wounds and conditioning	Continuous unconditional self love	Serving from unconditional love
Body	Recognizing the unity of body and being	Healing and transforming deep physical conditioning	Moving from body's unconditioned wisdom	Serving from deeply embodied Presence

© 2019 WholeBeing Awakening

	Singular		
© 2019 Whole Being Awakening	**13** Singular Realization	**14** Flow	**15** Unknown
	Dissolution of subject/object perspective	Life in fluid motion	Ongoing evolution
Consciousness	Awareness released from self-referencing	Awareness flows without resistance	?
Uniqueness	Personality expresses without attachment to sense of self	Free flowing personality	?
Mind	Thoughts happen without attachment to sense of self	Freely-flowing Intelligence	?
Emotions	Emotions happen without attachment to sense of self	Love in continuous flow	?
Body	Body moves without attachment to sense of self	Body flows freely through world	?

Development

Now let's more deeply explore development through the three Phases. We define development as growth toward maturity: becoming increasingly aware of, embodied in, and deeply living our potential in all Domains. Development in humans is similar to growth from seed to mature plant. It's about growing into what our whole being is designed to be. We experience development as the continuous urge to grow, evolve, mature, discover our uniqueness, find our place in human society, and fulfill our potential.

Human development is a whole-being process, so it's important not to get caught in any one of the Domains, thinking the others don't really matter. It's common to primarily focus on the Domains we feel most comfortable in, hoping to avoid the discomfort in whatever Domains may feel more challenging, traumatized, or less developed. The problem is, such avoidance causes even more pain than the discomfort of attending to the parts of ourselves that need extra love, support, attention, and healing. In our experience, attending to all Domains and Views while we develop, even if that feels like it's slowing you down, is what actually brings the fastest, most direct results.

It's important to mention the impact of trauma on human development. Trauma from obvious or subtle forms of neglect, abuse, or violence, plays a huge part in slowing or stunting development. The younger we are, the more impressionable we are, and the more easily we are conditioned by people and events around us. When our needs go unmet or when we are violated in any Domain, the result can be devastating and can hold back our evolution until the trauma is healed and integrated. People can suffer for years or decades if they grew up in an abusive environment. There is extensive research[14] that shows how abuse and neglect can be extremely challenging for the survival and health of the individual, both short and long term. If you find your development stuck at a less developed stage in one Domain vs. others, you might explore whether there is some trauma that needs healing or resolution.

We group Development into three major Phases: Dual, Unified, and Singular. The model further breaks each Phase into Stages, each of which describes a significant step of development. Please note that while development is related to age on average, we avoid suggesting any specific age correlations with Stages or Phases because we find such correlations fluid and changeable. Below is an overview of the 3 Phases of development.

Phase 1: Dual - Life and self are experienced as partial, fractured, confining, and disconnected

Early in the Dual Phase, life can be like looking through a keyhole, limiting our sight to small pieces of the scenery at a time. Most experience apparent splits between Domains simply because when we're young, we have limited capacity to hold many aspects of our experience together as a whole, inclusive reality. For example, some people are more aware of their body and less aware of their emotions until they are more developed. Sometimes we're more aware of thoughts but less aware of our consciousness. In Phase 1, it's common for there to be imbalances in how we develop in our Domains.

Another type of fracture is by Views. Some are far more focused on their own interior experience and have a hard time understanding how another person's view could be true or valid. Some are very focused on relationship and might find it difficult to value their own individual truth as much as that of others, or have a difficult time relating with, connecting, or working well with others. Still others tend to focus on observables (such as developing measurable skills), while ignoring what's going on inside. These are just a few examples of what we mean by the partial and fractured structure of awareness that characterizes the Dual Phase of development.

The Dual Phase also includes the tendency to see the world in pairs of opposites, like good vs. bad, big self vs. small self, true vs. false, real vs. unreal, right vs. wrong, etc. Although such divided and even polarized perspectives are incomplete as seen from more developed stages, it's important to understand that there's nothing wrong with the limits of any stage or phase. We need to first see life in parts before we can understand what it means to see life in unity and wholeness.

In the first 5 stages of Phase 1, we have a strong tendency to react against experiences we don't like. This can look like forcing, fixing, manipulating, lying, pretending, hiding, numbing, denying, ignoring, distracting, rejecting, improving, or blaming self and others... in short, doing anything but simply being present with discomfort. From our perspective, all of this is natural, based on our primary need to survive. The earlier we were forced to adopt strategies of resistance for our own survival, the more deeply we were conditioned by these patterns.

Most people are extremely conditioned by their experiences early in Phase 1. In Stage 4 we start to see this conditioning, and by Stage 6 we can feel how it amounts to a war with life and self. We see that we must come to terms with ourselves as we are and life as it is, not as we have idealized. In Stages 7 and 8, we begin to relax into life, and start letting go of our chronic forms of control and resistance.

Imagine you are given a jigsaw puzzle without the picture. Some pieces are right-side up, some upside down. To bring all the pieces together into their right place in the puzzle, you'd naturally start by examining each piece, grouping similar ones together, and making guesses about what the solution might look like. That's what living in Phase 1 is like; we naturally try to find the various parts of our own being and sort out how they fit together. Of course, it's not that the world is actually fractured like that, it's just that in Phase 1, we're not yet developed enough to be capable of perceiving the world in wholeness.

Whether we are aware of it or not, seeking to find the parts of who we are and how these parts are related to each other is a major theme in the Dual Phase. That very seeking impulse moves us to evolve and discover what is beyond our current horizons.

Phase 2: Unified - All Domains are known as whole, unified, and integrated

Entering the Unified Phase doesn't mean we are fully realized in our unified nature. It means there is a recognition of unification, and that recognition has started to dismantle the divided ways of seeing the world we were conditioned by in the Dual Phase.

In Phase 1, we try to sort out how all the pieces of life and self fit together. In Phase 2 it's as if there's a realization of the box top of your puzzle. You start to see how the parts of your being fit together and you start to experience the unity. Even when looking at the pieces, you begin to see the whole picture. You see that all pieces are unified with all other pieces. The experience is of a pervading sense of fundamental wholeness and whole-being wellness that was never present before. We realize that we are far greater than the sum of our parts.

Even with this remarkable change in our fundamental perception of self and life, this doesn't mean our perception is fully Singular because, in our analogy, the lines that appear to separate pieces are still there. We start feeling wholeness as the pieces fit together, but they still appear to be separate parts.

The Unified Phase starts with the realization of how infinite spaciousness and our personal, human self are connected. Unity also reveals the connections between self, others and the world. We start seeing the world from the 'both/and' perspective, feeling all dualities as connected and part of a larger whole. As we mature through the Unified Phase, we discover a deeper embodiment of unity through all the Domains of our being. We don't just realize, feel, and see the unity; we start to *live* it. Through living the unity realization, the edges that made us feel separate from ourselves and each other start to wear off. By the time we arrive at the end of the Unified Phase, we're ready to recognize the Singular nature of life.

Phase 3: Singular - *Dissolution of subject/object perspective*

The subject/object perspective is born of the sense that I am a subject here, somehow separate from people and objects I'm seeing over there. Because we were all deeply conditioned by the duality perspective as we grew up in Phase 1, the tendency to see the world that way is extremely persistent.

In the Unified Phase, we have realized that self and other are part of a single, universal reality. And yet, we still have the sense that we are a subject experiencing objects. But eventually, with appropriate support and understanding, we see past even the subtle assumptions of division that remain in the Unified Phase. As we move into the Singular Phase, the need to define ourselves as separate from the world evaporates. We start to feel so relaxed and anchored in the wholeness of our being that we find ourselves able to completely let go of the kinds of control and filters that we previously clung to. We find ourselves resting in the mystery of life and letting go of unnecessary control. This drops us into a fundamentally different perspective. We call it Singular because it's a recognition that no matter how separate things appear, what dominates is the awareness that life is living us.

In the Singular Phase, not only are the pieces put together, but the edges between pieces have dissolved, leaving one seamless experience of life – like the picture on the jigsaw puzzle box top. At this point, you are not relating to life as a puzzle to be solved; you are simply in the dance of life, being and doing what you are uniquely here to be and do. Life becomes a free flow in the fulfillment of your purpose.

Take a few minutes to read the stage headings and feel into what stage you think you may be in within each domain. This will give you an idea of where your growing edges are.

Domains

When we're young, it's obvious to us that development happens on a physical level because we can see and feel our bodies growing. It's harder to directly see development in other Domains, but we all know that development isn't limited to our bodies. Much emphasis is placed on mental and physical development in schools, whereas developing emotions and consciousness often lacks clear understanding or appropriate frameworks for growth and maturity. Also, support and encouragement for recognizing and living our unique gifts can be inconsistent, to say the least. The purpose of the iConscious model is to clearly show what it looks like for humans to grow in all 5 Domains and live our full potential.

We suggest that the totality of who we are individually is embraced in these five Domains and that all of them are crucial to our understanding of who we are in our whole being. While it's true that there are no hard boundaries between any of these Domains and that they are all intimately connected, using these five categories helps us to clearly discriminate the basic threads of our evolution. This ensures that all aspects of our being are included, tended to, and developed.

Consciousness

"Who would then deny that when I am sipping tea I am swallowing the whole universe with it?"
– Daisetz Teitaro Suzuki

We define Consciousness as the awareness that registers our experience. Please note that this is not the same thing as mind or thoughts. Consciousness is the transpersonal (beyond personal) end of the spectrum of life and self; it's the aspect of our experience that transcends who we are as individual human beings and connects us with all beings, life, and existence. It's the awareness that is aware of registering the words on this page. Consciousness is mysterious because it's invisible, yet intuitively known as an essential aspect of being human.

Consciousness can only be understood properly in the context of development. In the earlier stages, some intuit consciousness through the endless desire for something more, better, bigger, or deeper; something beyond the ordinary in our life. Others intuit consciousness through faith or religion. Some yearn for what transcends our sensory experience. Others come to know consciousness through a series of temporary yet life-altering experiences of infinite spaciousness, boundless love, or sublime mystery. In every case, what we mean by consciousness in Phase 1 is the recognition that, in addition to being this finite human person, we are also infinite spaciousness or presence. In Phase 2, consciousness is directly experienced as both self and other, both subject and object; it is recognized as non-separate from experience and as the unifying principle of all objects and experiences. In Phase 3, as subject/object experience dissolves into a singular reality, consciousness is experienced as the infinite mystery of life, indivisible from life itself.

Uniqueness

"Every human is like all other humans, some other humans, and no other human." – Clyde Kluckhon

The Uniqueness Domain includes all the ways each of us is unique, from our DNA to our personality and all the ways we think, feel and act. There are many systems for understanding type, or aspects of uniqueness, such as Myers-Briggs, the Enneagram, Strengths Based, or Jungian archetypes, etc. There are also many systems for typing bodies such as blood types, metabolic types, and Ayurvedic body types. Yet even when viewed through such lenses, our uniqueness can never be fully known by assessments of type – no matter how numerous or detailed – because each of us is unique and is therefore ultimately a mystery no matter how much we can know or understand.

You can think of uniqueness as the blueprint for how emotions, mind, and body express differently through you than through others. Uniqueness is like a seed that carries our essential qualities and tendencies. Some use the word "soul" to refer to the depth of our uniqueness.

In Phase 1, we seek to discover what makes us unique, then we learn to accept and embrace our uniqueness. This acceptance brings us into Phase 2, in which we learn to embody our authentic self and live our full potential unapologetically. In Phase 3, our unique essence flows into the world with no inner resistance to serve the needs of others.

Mind

"All that we are arises with our thoughts." –Buddha

The Mind Domain includes our relationship with our thoughts and beliefs, our capacity for mental complexity, and our ability to take in many perspectives, especially those that are not our own. Through most of Phase 1, our capacity for mental complexity is low, and we are unconsciously identified with our mind. Because we have limited perspective on our own mind, our capacity to understand others' mental realities is limited as well.

Toward the end of Phase 1, we see that mind is just a part of us. Instead of blindly believing our thoughts, we start to gain perspective on them, learning to question on our own thoughts and beliefs. In Phase 2, we see that our mind is an integral part of our whole-being nature, not separate from our body, emotions, uniqueness, or consciousness. We seek and find healing for the beliefs and mental patterns that no longer align with our authentic self. In Phase 3, our mind functions at its best, helping us navigate the mysteries of life with a style of functioning that avoids false divisions and reveals the connections between all things.

Emotions

"Your heart knows things that your mind can't explain."
– Vinith Kumar

The Emotions Domain includes our ability to feel and process the complexity of many emotional realities. This includes our energetic feelings and responses to life, such as love, anger, fear, joy, etc. All humans have access to the entire range of emotions. None of them are bad, and all of them provide information and tell us what matters to us uniquely. The more we honor and embrace our emotions (whether we like them or not), the more we can learn what they can teach us about who we are, and the more we can know our truth and bring our gifts into the world.

Remarkably, until Dan Goleman's 2005 book *Emotional Intelligence*, it seems that emotions were often not taken very seriously in academic or business settings, and were often considered something to be sublimated in many spiritual and religious traditions. The term EQ (vs. IQ) was barely know. In our experience, emotions are the heart of the matter. The house of our own body is not much of a home until we embrace our emotions and learn to enjoy and cooperate with them.

In Phase 1, we discover the range of our own emotions, struggle against the ones we don't like, then learn to accept and embrace them all. In Phase 2, we are drawn to heal our relationship with emotions and then fully align with them as we give ourselves to our unique purpose and function. In Phase 3, we no longer construct a sense of separate self from what we feel, which frees us to experience unrestricted emotional flow.

Body

"Take care of your body. It's the only place you have to live."
– Jim Rohn

The Body Domain is about our physical organism, including its structure, behavior, responses, processes, and movements, and all the ways we relate with our body. Our development in the Body Domain is primarily about how much we embrace and consciously embody our physical form and its natural functions.

In Phase 1, we tend to see our body as wrong, problematic, or something to manipulate, improve, or conquer. In Phase 2, it becomes obvious that our body is precious and its needs are deeply important. We also learn to deeply inhabit our body and see it as a seamless part of the world. In Phase 3, our body becomes the physical expression of the flow of life. We learn to let our body lead the way, knowing that our physical intuition is one of the most powerful assets we have.

Take a note of which Domain you feel you are most developed in and which one you feel most challenged in. Practice spending more time and attention in the Domains you usually avoid.

Whole-being lines

It's important to point out that many categories of evolution don't fit well into any of the above domains alone and are better thought of as "whole-being" lines of development that include all Domains together. For example, moral development isn't merely about what we're thinking; it also involves how we behave, what we feel, and how our personal uniqueness fits into our impact on others. Likewise, our development in faith, sexuality, esthetics, creativity, and material success involve all Domains. While it's beyond the scope of this book to trace such whole-being lines of development, we encourage you to consider how people grow in each Domain because that forms the basis of whole-being development.

Views

The third dimension in our framework is what we call Views, a concept based on the four quadrants from Ken Wilber's Integral theory. We've adapted this idea for our use and set forth our own definitions below.

Views are about what perspective we're taking. All of these views are accessible all the time, yet we're not always tuned into them. The more we learn to access all four Views, the more connected we are with our own experience, the experience of others, and the larger realities we live in.

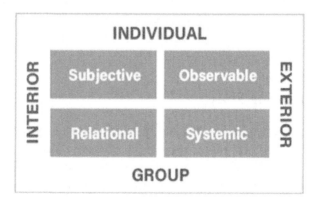

The diagram above shows how each View represents one corner of a box that includes Individual and Group, Interior and Exterior. You can see that Subjective View is about the interior of an individual, Observable is about the exterior of an individual, Relational is about sharing interior experiences in groups, and Systemic is about the exterior view of groups of individuals.

Subjective View

Subjective View represents a person's "inner terrain," including thoughts, feelings, sensations, and perceptions. This is about our personal experience of self, others and life. Because you are the only one living inside your own perspective, you probably have good access to this View. For most people, this means there's plenty of room to grow by putting attention on the other 3 Views. As we grow in the Subjective View, we become more and more aware of the details of our inner reality, and we learn to embrace them, whether we consider them positive or negative.

- Practice accessing the Subjective View by tracking your inner reality. Go into your day paying attention to what you think, what you feel emotionally, and what you sense in your body.
- Journal about the patterns of thoughts, emotions, and physical sensations that you experience while watching your inner reality. The more you understand

your own inner patterns, the more you know about who you are (including what's innate and what's conditioned), and what matters to you.
- Look for your inner response system. Most people are designed to feel how to respond in a situation because something inside says "this feels good," "this feels bad," or "this doesn't evoke much response from me". The more in touch you are with these feelings, the more you can respond to life's endless choices in ways that are truly aligned with who you are.

Observable View

The Observable View includes everything others can perceive about you by using their own senses or any type of device such as a camera or heart rate monitor. Things that are observable include your appearance, actions, expressions, skills, and medical information such as EEG, DNA, or MRI results. As we grow in the Observable View, we become increasingly open to and interested in what can be perceived about us from the outside and how that relates to our inner experience.

- Practice accessing the Observable View by paying attention to what others can perceive or detect about you. This includes how you look, dress, and behave. How open are you to hearing about how others see you?
- Journal about this question: Is there a reason I avoid putting attention on my own exterior? If so, why?
- Practice asking others you trust what they observe about you. Notice how you feel when receiving this feedback.
- Observable View includes medical test results and things doctors can perceive about your body and its functioning. Do you have any resistance to this type of feedback? If so, why?

Relational View

The Relational View is about the interior experiences of our relationships with others and groups, such as shared feelings, experiences, meanings, values, culture, and ideas. We engage the Relational view when we work or play with others and when we engage in social media through computers, TV, and radio. As we develop in the Relational View, we become less self-centered, more aware of others' realities, and more sensitive to the needs of the others we're relating with. We also become more capacble of feeling whatever shows up in relationship.

> • Practice accessing the Relational View by paying attention to what happens between you and others. Pay more attention than usual to the feelings that move between you and those you are relating with. These feelings are often much more important than what's being said.
> • Journal about how you protect or defend yourself when relating with others, and why. Also write about how this defense system is working for you, especially in the relationships that matter most to you. What do you gain by defending? What do you lose by defending?

Systemic View

The Systemic View represents what can be perceived, studied, and understood about collectives such as physical, economic, organizational, political, structural, or natural systems. The Systemic view includes groups, businesses, nations, economies, roads, buildings, governments, forests, oceans, and galaxies. As we grow in the Systemic View, we become increasingly aware of the larger systems we live in, how we are related to them, how we impact those systems, and how those systems impact us.

- Practice gaining access to the Systemic View by paying attention to the structures and behaviors of naturally occurring and human systems in the world around you. Do these seem less important than what's happening inside yourself?
- What's more important to you: Your experience of your health, or research and understandings about health? If you're more focused on your subjective experience of health, see if you have any objections to exploring understandings that others have developed about health.
- Join meetings (at work if applicable) with colleagues who are thinking and planning at a higher strategic level, even just to observe and absorb. This will expose you to ways of seeing how systems of people function and are connected with each other.

Access to Views

It's important to understand that all four Views exist simultaneously and are accessible in every moment. But most of us are in the habit of attending to one or two of these far more often than the others. The result of avoiding or disconnecting from other perspectives include:

- Primary focus on subjective thoughts, feelings, and experiences makes it harder to connect with or feel compassion for others. It also tends to exclude awareness of how others observe you, what's happening in the "we-space," and how you are interacting with larger social and environmental systems. Exclusive focus on subjective experience will limit growth because, despite the illusion of separation, we are all part of each other and the larger systems in which we live.
- Primary focus on how others see us makes it easy to neglect our personal experience and lose track of our own body It also limits our ability to experience relational realities and the larger systems we're part of.
- Primary focus on relationships can make it easy to ignore our subjective truth and miss basic things that can be observed, including the systems that provide the context for our relationships.
- Primary focus on systems such as politics or the environment can lead to ignore ourselves, our relationships, and the individual people and things we can see that matter as much as the systems they are part of.

To illustrate the importance of considering all Views, imagine a man has built his house on the edge of a river. All is well until there is a flood, which destroys his home. A little extra awareness of the natural systems he's part of could have avoided that disaster! Now imagine the man rebuilds the house in a safer place. Again, all is well until his wife leaves him because he spent too much time working. Some extra attention to the importance of his relationship might have prevented that heartache. Think about your own life... which of the four Views have you tended to avoid? What's been the impact of that?

We observe that the more open we are to what's happening in all Views, the faster we develop and the more effective we are at everything we do. Taking all four Views into consideration can help us reduce our blind spots and integrate faster. As we expand our awareness to include all Views, our own evolution accelerates because we are no longer ignoring important aspects of life.

- Journal: Is there a View that you tend to spend more time and attention in? For instance, do you tend to spend more of your time and attention on what you are thinking, feeling, needing, or wanting? Do you have a tendency to avoid your own experience and focus on how others see you? Do you tend to fixate on relationship dynamics? Do you spend most of your time studying systems? Please note which Views you spend the most time in, and which you tend to avoid, or feel are not very developed.
- Practice by spending more time attending to the Views you usually neglect or avoid.

States and stages

Starting in Section 3, we describe each stage of development in our model. It's important to understand the distinction between stages and states. States are temporary, short-term experiences. We experience constant fluctuations of state, as we move from feeling energetic, to tired, to happy, to sad, to blissful, etc. What we mean by a stage is a lasting, long-term platform that underlies our changing states. Each stage we describe in our model has its own values and ways of viewing the world that persist usually for months or years. For example, you might experience a flow state for some hours, in which you feel completely absorbed in a creative project, and then later you may feel out of flow (perhaps absorbed in confusion or mental chatter). By contrast, when you evolve to Stage 14, you experience flow as the constant, underlying basis of your life and everything you do. Flow becomes your moment-to-moment everyday way of being in the world.

It can often be valuable to learn to change our state to regulate or resource ourselves. State changes can be induced many ways, including through practices, techniques, experiences in nature, food, substances, even movies. But even temporary experiences of more developed stages aren't the same as living in those stages. Temporary states that give us experience of our own more developed stages are important; they open us in ways that help our system harmonize toward our next way of functioning. But manipulating our states can easily become a detour, leading to an endless grasping for preferable experiences.

It's important to understand that more evolved stages are not attained by willfully changing ourselves to get what we want. In our experience, we evolve most quickly when we learn to deeply accept and embrace the endless alternations of states while consistently fulfilling our needs at each stage.

Shadow

We define shadow as aspects of self that are currently hidden from awareness, including painful memories and conditioned patterns, which typically include various unwanted emotions. From one perspective, the entire human development process is one of consciously bringing parts of ourselves from shadows (unconscious) into light (conscoius). We find it most effective to not resist or vilify what is in the shadow. What works best is to look for what is just beyond what you can currently see, and do your best to embrace whatever you encounter. It's all present and waiting to be embraced at some point. By accepting the fact that there is always more to be seen, we reduce our resistance to life, which in turn supports our deeper development.

About Ego

We find that most people who are interested in personal and/or consciousness development have run across the idea of ego. Many have gotten the idea that ego is something that needs to be defeated or overcome. The result is that they end up in a battle with themselves. How can you win a war with yourself? In our experience, you can't.

Some think of ego as a separate entity, because they associate ego with an inner narrative that is focused on them. While it's easy to think of ego as if it were a separate entity, we don't find that framing helpful. From our perspective, ego is not a separate thing, nor is it who we are. We think of it as a pattern of thoughts, beliefs, and feelings that give us a partial or temporary *sense* of self. This partial sense of self is important because it drives us to realize our *whole* self. We know intuitively that who we are is not limited to these patterns.

Although this may sound counterintuitive, we find that what helps us to get beyond ego is to start by accepting that these patterns are here. This doesn't mean we like them, nor that we need to indulge them, just that we need to accept them because they are part of our current reality. Accepting these patterns frees up the energy that was being wasted on the battle against them and allows us to drop into who we are right now, versus who we wish we were. This embrace of the truth of our current self prompts the realization of unity because we are no longer separating ourselves from these parts of self.

Embodied Unity opens awareness to wholeness, including awareness of our whole self. In the Unified Phase, our sense of self is whole and inclusive; it's both universal and personal as one. At this point, it's important to surround ourselves with people who will feed back any egoic self-inflation that may occur. It's one thing to realize the truth of our own infinite wholeness, but it's another thing to think that makes us better than others.

By the time we evolve to the Singular Phase, there is no further need for a sense of self. The patterns we used to think of as ego may still exist, but they are dwarfed by the infinite magnificence of life. We still exist, but we no longer need to generate mental or other activities to affirm a separate or limited sense of self.

From a larger perspective, ego can be seen as a kind of protective cocoon that helps us feel safe so we can develop.

This cocoon grows with us, becoming a larger and larger space for us to evolve into. As we reach whole-being maturity, we shed the cocoon and live without need for any barrier between ourselves and the world.

Stage Overviews

Starting in Section 3, we introduce each stage with information that pertains to all Domains in that stage. These include Stage Overview statements for all 4 Views, along with descriptions, needs, images, quotes, and practices. In the stage summaries in Stages 1-12, we have also added statements that describe how a person identifies their sense of self at that stage. We don't offer identities from Stage 13 on because at that point, we have evolved beyond the need for a personally constructed sense of self.

What's in each Location

Beneath each Stage Overview, we write about the primary features of each Location in the model. Below is a description of what's included.

Location Description

At the top of each location, you'll see the short Location Description also shown on the model. Please be aware that the short descriptions we offer here cannot possibly cover all the subtleties of each location and should be taken only as examples.

Needs

The famous psychologist Abraham Maslow observed that there is a hierarchy of needs each person must find ways to fulfill in order to grow and unfold their full potential. He described those needs as physical (food, water, warmth, safety and security) and psychological (self-esteem, belonging, intimacy). When the "lower" needs are met, he observed that the "higher" needs of creativity, self-actualization, and self-transcendence naturally follow. We agree, and we find that this progression of needs doesn't stop. In other words, it's not like a triangle or pyramid with an apex because there is no final or ultimate pinnacle of human development.

When our survival needs have been sufficiently met in Stage 1, we quickly evolve into Stage 2, etc. Fulfilling the needs at any stage results in rapid development into the next stage. By connecting with the needs and finding what works uniquely for you to fulfill them, growth toward deep self-realization and actualization proceeds most directly. Because this is such an important point, we've listed needs in each location of the model. The needs we've listed are the ones that when fulfilled will help move us from the start of the current Stage to the middle of it and beyond.

We should also mention that sometimes some of our needs are met, and others are not. The result can be that parts of us move into the next stage and other parts get left behind, causing shadow issues to develop.

Images & Quotes

In each location, we offer an image and a quote to help you understand the essential meaning. We put them there to help illustrate the flavor of the location that we're talking about. These are only examples; feel free to find your own images and quotes that represent the meanings we describe.

Longer Description

Below the image and quote is a longer description of the current location. This will give you an understanding of the main features of development in this area and how we evolve toward the next location.

Practices

Practices are important tools for accelerating our evolution. They give us specific ways to stretch ourselves in directions appropriate for our growing edges. We have added suggested practices in each location for Stages 1-12, but not beyond that because in Phase 3, people are far less impelled to direct their attention to themselves. As with the needs, the practices we offer are designed to support your development from the start of the current stage to the middle of it and beyond.

The practices offered are suggestions and examples; hopefully they will inspire you to find whatever practices work best for you and your unique needs. We encourage you to try any practices that feel relevant to you, regardless of their position in our model. The positions we placed them in here are derived from averages, and no one is average.

Growing Organically

Reaching for higher development is natural, but it's important to understand that we cannot skip stages; we must fulfill the needs of whatever stage we are in before more developed stages can emerge and stabilize.

Similar to a tree growing, each new stage is predicated on the foundations built in the prior stages. It's impossible for a tree to develop branches if the trunk is not established. And it's impossible for flowers to grow if the branches, twigs and leaves are not developed. Similarly, we humans cannot experience a full range of physical functions until our bodies have matured. Nor can we have a full range of mental or emotional functions until the cognitive and limbic parts of our brain have developed. In that way, each Stage of development can only follow after the previous one.

Development is also nested, because each stage of

development not only brings new capacities, but also includes the capacities of the previous Stages. Just because a tree flowers doesn't mean it stopped having roots and branches. And when a human develops new capacities, they retain the previous ones. This is what is meant by the phrase "transcend and include." We bring this up because we find many get confused when they continue to experience parts of themselves they thought they outgrew or went beyond. Our point is that we can never get beyond any part of who we are; we simply become less limited by our previous perspectives and we become increasingly inclusive.

As we grow, we notice the limits of our current location, which often motivates us to grow toward the next one. It's been our observation that, while most people develop in the order shown in the model, some appear to jump ahead and bounce back as they evolve, resulting in apparent gaps in horizontal development. If that's your pattern, nothing is wrong. Almost everyone experiences temporary states that represent both earlier and later stages from our current average location in any domain. And some people even appear to stabilize "later" stages before "earlier" ones. While this may appear to violate the principle of "transcend and include", we find that from a larger perspective, it's as natural as the impossible-to-predict locations of electrons spinning around a nucleus. Especially from Stage 7 on, we find that human evolution displays those kinds of quantum properties.

Section 3:
Developing in the Dual Phase

"Every explicit duality is an implicit unity." – Alan Watts

The following sections are devoted to describing the experience, needs, and helpful practices in each Domain at each Stage, starting with the stage in the Dual Phase. We recommend reading all sections, not just the ones you feel speak to where you are right now. Understanding the entire range of development will help you understand the context of your current experience in the larger scope of your life and will help keep your development moving in the right direction. It will also inspire you with the possibilities of what your life can be like.

The Dual Phase includes Stages 1-8 in the model. In Phase 1, we experience life and self as partial, fractured, confining, and disconnected. We can feel separate from ourselves and from others, lost, or confused about who we are and what we're doing here. There is often a sense of searching for oneself, along with a felt sense of something missing, lacking, or not enough. In the earlier part of the Dual Phase, life is seen as filled with conflicting polarities, such as good versus bad, right versus wrong, me versus you, us versus them, etc. Toward the end of Phase 1, we begin to see and accept the "both/and" and fluid gray zones of life. We yearn for an end to our suffering, our war with self and life, and a unification of our personal self with transpersonal nature, which is finally fulfilled in Phase 2.

The Dual Phase is a time for seeking and discovering who we are and what life is, piece by piece, while those pieces start slowly fitting themselves together in our awareness. During this Phase, our general disposition evolves from resisting life and self (by fixing, changing, improving, or avoiding) to fundamentally embracing everything, including what we don't like. Evolving from fundamentally rejecting life to embracing it sets us up for the Unified Phase, in which we discover that, despite appearances, the various parts of our being were never separate in the first place.

Stage 1: Survival

Stage Overview: Primary focus on staying alive

- Subjective: Absorbed in surviving
- Observable: Instinctive survival behaviors
- Relational: Completely dependent on others
- Systemic: Interacting instinctively with systems

Needs: To be safe and nurtured with warmth, food, love, and bonding

Identity: I'm dependent on others

"We don't even know how strong we are until we are forced to bring that hidden strength forward. In times of tragedy, of war, of necessity, people do amazing things."
— Isabel Allende

In Stage 1, as infants, we are dependent on caregivers for our survival. Our primary need is to bond with caregivers and receive primal nurturance. This need becomes less toward the end of Stage 1, freeing us to explore the world more.

As adults we experience Stage 1 when we are too ill,

injured, or compromised to care for ourselves, or when we have temporary states of survival issues or fears. Examples include emotional, physical, and financial circumstances. Big stressors in any Domain or View can appear to reverse our evolution no matter what stage we are in. For example, losing your job may seem to bring you back into survival-mode, however this is a temporary state, not a stage shift.

Living on the edge of survival leaves few inner resources available for larger perspectives. Everything feels reduced to immediate needs. At this stage, we have limited awareness of other Domains outside whichever one(s) are compromised, and we are primarily focused in the Subjective View. What we need most is air, food, warmth, protection, and nurturance. We need to live without threat, injury, or violation.

Especially when we are young, and our needs for safety, sustenance, love, and bonding are not well met, our development is hindered. The unmet needs can grow into shadow issues that negatively affect every aspect of our lives. As wounds and traumas are incurred and needs go unfulfilled, coping strategies increase and unconscious beliefs may form, such as "I can't trust anyone". This is why a huge key to healthy development is healthy caregivers who can help us fulfill our needs in a loving way.

Whatever wounds and traumas occur, the sooner they are felt, loved, and healed, the better. Even deep wounds can heal as we find the right types of support and nurturance. As soon as we have sufficient free energy and attention to fend for ourselves, we start doing whatever we must to insure our survival as a platform for further development.

Please keep in mind that as we grow, we "transcend and include," so we never get away from our survival needs in all Domains no matter what stage of development we are living in.

Gary: When I lost my job, it freaked me out because I had no way to pay my bills. So I worked really hard to find a new job, and I got one that took care of my needs.

- You have a right to exist. Honor yourself by doing whatever is necessary to get what you need to live so you can grow.
- When others offer to help you, accept their support.
- Learn to ask for support.

Stage 1 – Consciousness

Location Description: Attention focused on immediate needs

Needs: To be at the center of caregivers' attention. Until this need is met, the individual will naturally yearn to find someone who can model loving presence.

"Without self-awareness we are as babies in the cradles."
– Virginia Woolf

Consciousness is the transpersonal aspect of our being. It's that part of us that is aware of and registers our experience that we share with all beings and things in the universe. In western cultures, Consciousness is often the last Domain to come online. Most people are relatively unaware of their own consciousness until at least Stage 5 or, more often, Stage 7 when consciousness begins to awaken to itself. Most people acquire ideas about what Consciousness is, but lack direct experience of it until later in the Dual Phase.

In Stage 1, we are not very aware of or present to the world outside of ourselves. We have little awareness and therefore little self-awareness. Lacking perspective on ourselves makes it hard for us to understand how others see us, or why they respond to us as they do. It also makes it impossible for us to understand ourselves or what we are doing in this life. People at this stage can feel lost and often appear lost to others. It's as if the lights are barely on in one's inner world.

Emma: I spent years feeling like I was on automatic, just doing things because I was supposed to. I don't even think I know how lost I felt; all I knew was that something felt wrong about my life and I didn't know how to fix it.

- It's ok to need attention. Ask for the attention you need and when you get it, take it in.
- Give yourself attention. Become aware of yourself by noticing what you think, feel, and do.

Stage 1 – Uniqueness

Location Description: Uniqueness expressed unconsciously

Needs: To be supported for who we are

*"You are obligated to understand that you are unique
in the world. There has never been anyone like you because,
if there were, there would be no need for you to exist.
You are an utterly new thing in creation. Your
life goal is to realize this uniqueness." – Aaron Perlow*

In Stage 1, we have little or no awareness of our personal uniqueness. Under ideal conditions, those around us will see, value, and reflect our unique qualities so we can eventually see them for ourselves. It usually takes many further stages of development before we can consciously see and embrace our own uniqueness. Even while we are unaware of our unique needs, if they are not met, or if our needs are violated, the impact can be deep and lasting, at least until there is healing. Simply not being seen for our unique needs, gifts, and tendencies will naturally make us feel unseen and unmet, even invisible.

Liam: For most of the earlier part of my life, I had no idea what I wanted. I just wanted what would make other people happy. Eventually I realized I was scared of being rejected if what I wanted was different from those around me.

- Tune into your personal needs and wants. Find ways to get your unique needs met in ways that work for you.
- Explore what makes you unique. When others suggest what's unique about your gifts or limits, see if it feels true to you.

Stage 1 – Mind

Location Description: Thinking occupied with survival needs

Needs: To have our needs understood

"In the egoic state, your sense of self, your identity, is derived from your thinking mind ... what your mind tells you about yourself." – Eckhart Tolle

In Stage 1, thoughts can appear magically real, almost like external objects. They are extremely compelling to our attention and make us feel like our thoughts are who we are in our fundamental identity. This leads to a tendency in the Dual Phase to believe our own thoughts without question and to be completely absorbed in them. There's a tendency to exclusively identify our sense of self with our thoughts. This can reduce our awareness in other Domains and contribute to a sense of division within ourselves, and between self, others, and world.

Carl: I used to spend all my time in my imagination, thinking about stories I wanted to write. Eventually, I ran out of money and had to get a job doing physical work. At first I hated it, but then I realized it got me out of my head and it actually made me feel better.

- Notice your thoughts. Become aware of when your attention is more in your mind versus in your emotions or physical sensations.
- When you don't need to be thinking, practice bringing your attention to your body. What's it like to live life from a place other than from thinking?

Stage 1 – Emotions

Location Description: Survival-based instinctive emotional reactions

Needs: To be loved unconditionally

"Our emotions are the driving powers of our lives."
– Earl Riney

Emotions are feeling sensations that often contain information about what matters to us. At the start of Stage 1, emotions can feel so powerful that they feel bigger than our sense of self, and we are often challenged to cope with them. Emotions can often feel overwhelming and more than we can handle. Later, usually starting in Stage 7, we realize that we are bigger than our own emotions, which allows us to begin finding a healthier relationship with them.

In the earlier parts of the Dual Phase, we are often unable to discriminate our emotions from the rest of ourselves. Emotions can feel like they engulf us, or they *are* us. When emotions are strong, it can be hard to connect with a sense of self beyond what we are feeling. In these earlier stages, we often see from and as the emotions versus having the capacity to also look at them. Our sense of self can become fused with emotions, with no space between or around them. It can also be difficult to discriminate emotional emergencies from physical ones.

Especially when we're young, when those around us don't meet us in our emotions (such as when certain feelings are disallowed or made wrong), it's hard for us to learn how to behave with our own emotions. Shadow zones (unmet and unseen parts of us) can begin to grow, causing increasing rifts between self and other. To the degree we are not unconditionally loved, we tend to develop the feeling "there is something wrong with me". Our need to be loved is so strong, that we can abandon parts of ourselves to get love from others.

In the Dual Phase, because of resistance to emotions and lack of emotional development, we often create dramas that take over our life. In the attempt to feel safe, we can build emotional walls in our relationships. Some people spend their entire lives unconsciously avoiding certain feelings from arising while focusing on preferred feelings. While it's important to move toward happiness, avoidance of emotional pain and discomfort tends to cause a lot of extra pain in both the short and long term. It can also cause us to make decisions informed by fear, rather than openness and curiosity. Embracing whatever emotions we feel characterizes the more mature stages of development.

Abby: I used to have big anger issues. I was angry about almost everything and I always assumed it was because other people were doing things that were making me mad. Years later I realized I was conditioned to suppress my anger, and that's why I was always angry! I also realized nobody can "make" me feel anything. My inner state is my responsibility. It isn't up to anyone but me. It was so eye opening to realize how much I was giving my power away by blaming others for my own experience.

- Connect with your emotions by putting your attention on them.
- Honor your emotions by finding ways to get your emotional needs met.
- Journal about a situation that you find upsetting. What are your feelings saying?

Stage 1 – Body

Location Description: Instinctive survival-based physical reactions

Needs: To be safe, protected, and nurtured with food, clothing, warmth, shelter, medicines, and survival technologies

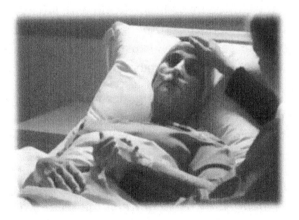

*"Our body is precious. It is our vehicle for awakening.
Treat it with care." – Buddha*

As infants, our bodies are extremely vulnerable and needy. We must be constantly attended to, and our needs must be met for us to survive. If our physical needs are not well supported by our caregivers, we may fail to thrive. If we survive, we may feel endlessly needy until we find ways to truly fulfill our needs. We can also become dissociated from our body, and try to compensate from whatever Domain we feel safe to inhabit. This degrades our health and makes it hard to feel comfortable in our own skin. It also makes us less comfortable functioning in the physical world.

As adults, we can revisit Stage 1 as a temporary state any time we are physically injured or violated, or when our body's needs are unmet. For example, having low blood sugar can bring us back to our immediate need for food. If our physical needs were violated when young, then as adults we might have PTSD, low body awareness, or other conditions that can leave us vulnerable to sickness or injury. In Stage 1, we often move in the world with little awareness of our physical impact on others, or others' impact on us. In Stage 1, our sense of self is usually fused with our body, leaving little room for awareness of our other Domains.

We also need to survive energetically; each of us has our own needs for space, rest, relaxation, and finding our own rhythms. The sooner we learn how to fulfill these needs, the less issues we suffer in our adult lives.

Amy: After my accident, I was unable to care for myself for almost 4 months. I was so grateful my sister was able to care for me.

- Honor your body's needs by noticing them and finding ways to fulfill them.
- When you can't fulfill your own physical needs, ask for help. When help is offered, accept it.

Stage 2: Self-Centric

Stage Overview: Impuliksve and self absorbed

- Subjective: Strengthening boundaries of the separate self
- Observable: Tendency toward impulsive behavior
- Relational: Minimal awareness of others' reality, value, or perspectives
- Systemic: Interacting based on power dynamics

Needs: To get what I want

Identity: I'm a separate person

"Self-centered leaders manipulate for personal benefit.
Mature leaders motivate for mutual benefit."
— John C. Maxwell

As toddlers In Stage 2, what little awareness we have is absorbed in our subjective world. We act on impulse because we have not learned to accept limits, discipline, or the need for self-control. Our need to be validated with positive feedback and attention makes us believe we should be the center of everyone's world. In this stage, we have challenges distinguishing our needs, realities, and beliefs from those of others. We also have very low awareness of our impact on others because most attention is on self. The low impulse control at this stage affects others, who bring us lessons about social interaction.

As adults, we can experience temporary states in which the qualities of Stage 2 dominate. This can be especially true when we're deeply stressed or feel unsupported and feel forced to make ourselves the top priority.

Jenny: Looking back, I can see where I was completely unable to take in anyone else's perspective or be very concerned about other's needs. It wasn't out of lack of care; it was just that I couldn't see past my own needs.

- It's deeply important for us to know that we matter. Ask someone who cares about you to tell you why you matter and why you are special. Everyone is special, and everyone needs to know why.
- When someone gives you praise, practice consciously letting it in without deflecting.

Stage 2 – Consciousness

Location Description: Awareness absorbed in one's own immediate wants

Needs: To discover a sense of self awareness

"The ultimate value of life depends upon awareness ... rather than upon mere survival." – Aristotle

Those in Stage 2 are not very self-aware. When someone doesn't get feedback and support to develop self-awareness, they can continue to evolve in other Domains, yet still be absorbed in their own world.

As consciousness grows in us, it can appear in many ways. Sometimes it dawns in a way that makes people feel like they're being watched, and they may misinterpret consciousness to be their "conscience," a set of moral ideas, which we classify as part of the Mind domain.

Charlie: As a young kid, I had experiences of feeling like I was being witnessed by a heavenly host. There was just this feeling of being watched, as if I was the subject of a movie. Looking back on it, I can see that was my own consciousness starting to come online.

- Sit quietly and allow your awareness to expand into the space around you. Notice the sense of existing in a larger field of awareness.
- When you discover something about yourself you weren't previously aware of, journal about it. Writing down your observations will help you integrate the new parts you discover.

Stage 2 – Uniqueness

Location Description: Limited awareness of the value of my uniqueness

Needs: To be seen and supported in one's own unique personality and ways of being in the world

"One of the most important gifts a parent can give a child is the gift of accepting that child's uniqueness." – Fred Rogers

As children, we have all kinds of amazing gifts, but it usually takes us years to recognize the value of our uniqueness. In the earlier stages of development, it's easy to look at others, see how we're different, and assume something is wrong either with ourselves or with others. This is especially true when those we look up to don't show us how to deal with our own uniqueness. The sooner we get support to value our uniqueness, the sooner we can be ok with who we are, with being different from others, and with others being different from us.

Margo: I was so identified with my friends that I had trouble seeing what was unique about me. I actually didn't want to be different; I just wanted to belong. But years later I had to leave that group just so I could find myself.

- Do you have the sense that there's something wrong with your unique self? Journal about what you think is wrong.
- Next, journal about what might be right or amazing about your uniqueness.

Stage 2 – Mind

Location Description: Absorption in one's own thoughts

Needs: To discriminate what thoughts to act on

"Humanity is mind-controlled and only slightly more conscious than your average zombie."– David Icke

In this stage, we tend to be fused with our mind, with limited awareness of our thought patterns and their impact on self and others. You can see this in little kids when they spontaneously express themselves in ways others consider inappropriate This can also be seen in adults who don't have much perspective on their own mind; thoughts can be spoken or acted upon without considering the consequences in the given context.

Sarah: When I was younger, I used to say horrible things to people to get them out of my space. I didn't intend to hurt anyone, I just felt overwhelmed and I didn't know how hurtful I was really being.

Norman: I made an impulsive decision to approve a budget that caused the company to lose thousands of dollars. Looking back, I can see I was blind to the bigger picture and was serving my own needs.

- Spend time observing your thoughts without acting on them.
- Journal about what patterns you see in your thoughts.
- Notice how these thought patterns show up in your daily life, and the impact they have.

Stage 2 – Emotions

Location Description: Emotionally self-absorbed

Needs: To become aware of one's own emotions

"It would be impossible to estimate how much time and energy we invest in trying to fix, change and deny our emotions – especially the ones that shake us at our very core, like hurt, jealousy, loneliness, shame, rage and grief." – Debbie Ford

At this stage, we tend to impulsively act out our emotions. There is limited awareness of what's driving this; we are simply immersed in our feelings without noticing that some of our behaviors are actually reactions against uncomfortable feelings. People around us can be more aware of our emotions than we are; in any case, they are usually much more aware of the impact our emotions are having on them. In this stage we can feel intensely unhappy or elated, yet not know why. There's a tendency toward reactivity, along with not noticing one's impact on others.

Sara: Even though I had plenty of emotional outbursts, I was not very aware of what I was feeling or what I needed emotionally. People walked on egg shells around me, unsure when I might explode.

- Journal about your experiences and how they make you feel.
- Spend time during your day consciously attending to your emotions by simply feeling them without acting on them.

Stage 2 – Body

Location Description: Exclusive focus on satisfying physical wants

Needs: To learn the impact of our physical behaviors on ourselves and others

"When you're young … you're acting on impulse, which is very important and valuable. But you're kind of swimming in a blind sea. When you get older, you have more of a sense of direction." – Sinead O'Connor

Most people exhibit impulsive or reactive behavior once in a while, but at Stage 2, impulsive action is the norm. Impulsivity is the tendency to act on a whim, displaying behavior characterized by little or no forethought, reflection, or consideration of the consequences. Impulsive actions are typically poorly conceived, prematurely expressed, unduly risky, or inappropriate to the situation that often result in undesirable consequences, which imperil long-term goals and strategies for success.

Jeremy: As a young adult, I was very rebellious. I even went to jail for doing something dumb just because it felt incredibly compelling in that moment. Since then, I've learned not to act out like that.

- Spend time noticing your own impulses and actions. See if you can feel the tendency to act based on a feeling you don't like.
- Journal about the effects acting on impulse has had on those around you.
- When you feel impulsive, practice not acting on your feelings.

Stage 3: Conforming

Stage Overview: Conforming to identity group

- Subjective: Modeling those in identity group to fit in
- Observable: Loyal compliance with rules while resisting outsiders
- Relational: Relating to others as modeled by group norms
- Systemic: Interacting based on authority

Needs: To feel support and belonging

Identity: I belong to my identity group

"A deep sense of love and belonging is an irreducible need of all people. We are … wired to love, to be loved, and to belong. When those needs are not met, we don't function as we were meant to." – Brene Brown

In the conforming Stage, there is a tendency toward compliance with the rules of the group while resisting outsiders. Some are more loyal to the group, others are more rebellious, but either way in Stage 3, we must align ourselves enough with those around us to get our needs met and to grow. In doing so, we learn to reduce impulsive behavior to be accepted in family, team, society and culture. When children are raised by parents who don't teach them limits, they can grow up with poor impulse control, which causes a lot of problems in life.

In Stage 3, we learn how to follow. We follow our parents, teachers, company leaders, and religious leaders. We learn from others by mimicking them and seeing what works for us. We learn to follow before we can effectively lead.

On the down side, the need to belong is so strong it can drive us to give up or ignore parts of our truth. At this stage, it's common to deny who we are, what we're thinking, or what we're feeling from a fear of lack of acceptance. But as we develop, fulfill our needs to belong, and become more independent, we become less willing to betray ourselves to be part of family, business, or any particular group.

Melissa: For a while, I felt safe playing by the rules. Although a rebel and free-spirit at heart, I learned how others – mostly my family, work, and church – wanted me to behave. I learned that if I wanted to be accepted, respected, and loved, I needed to think, talk, and act a certain way, even if that meant squelching parts of me. Although I felt safe and a part of the group, over time I also felt confined.

- Journal about your judgment of or avoidance of outsiders or people who are different from you. Do you feel strong aversions or negative emotions towards certain types of people?
- Journal about the commonalities between you and the person or types of people you have an aversion to.

Stage 3 – Consciousness

Location Description: Awareness developing within the limits of identity group

Needs: To conform to caregivers' expectations of how consciousness appears

"Each of us is a unique thread woven into the beautiful fabric of our collective consciousness." – Jaeda DeWalt

In Stage 3 we tend to conform to the rules and expectations of the groups we are part of. On one hand, the fact that we are conditioned by those around us is a good thing; it gives us a template and a starting point for consciousness development. On the other hand, the pressure to conform limits our consciousness development to what is permissible by the group. If you are part of a religious tradition, your first experiences of consciousness may have a similar religious frame. If you're a part of a mystical tradition, consciousness may develop as a mystical thing for you. If you didn't grow up with any modeling around developing awareness, you may find yourself seeking people who can model higher stages of consciousness so you can begin to explore this important Domain of your own being. If your experience of consciousness doesn't match those around you, your development in this Domain may be delayed due to lack of support.

By the end of Stage 3, we feel the urge to break out of whatever boxes and expectations we were previously limited by. We may start having experiences of consciousness in forms we couldn't previously allow.

Roger: I used to have mystical experiences that were actually frowned upon in my religion. Years later, although it was hard, I left that context and started having experiences of consciousness that were supported and encouraged by my new friends.

- Journal about your experience of consciousness, God, or universal presence.
- Write about how these experiences are similar to or different from others in your family, church, or others around you.

Stage 3 – Uniqueness

Location Description: Recognizing uniqueness acceptable to identity group

Needs: To get support to become who and what I am here to be

"The hardest thing I've ever done is to find where I belong."
– Jess Hudak

Because we need the support of our family, friends, and teachers, our developing uniqueness can easily get stifled while we're busy trying to fit in. When we need to be a part of a group, yet sense that certain parts of our uniqueness are not accepted there, we will often stifle those parts in order to meet our needs for safety and belonging.

This plays out in our relationship with family members because that's where our deepest needs are fulfilled (or not) when we are growing up. Learning to conform when we are young helps us learn how to find our place in life, but it can simultaneously challenge us to discover our own authenticity. As adults, it's very important to find out who we are uniquely and what inspires us to work and be creative. Until that happens, life can feel meaningless.

Madison: I think my biggest challenge is figuring out why I'm here or what I'm good for. I can do a lot of things, but none of them feel meaningful. I like being part of my team at work, but I still don't know what I really want to be or do.

- Journal – What do you want to explore that may not be acceptable to your family, friends, or coworkers?
- Journal – What do you hide about yourself from your family or identity group?
- Contemplate – If you could do anything you want, what would it be? What would be fun for you?

Stage 3 – Mind

Location Description: Only allowing thoughts and beliefs acceptable to identity group

Needs: To think within identity group limits

"Why does your mind conform? Have you ever asked? Are you aware that you are conforming to a pattern?"
– J. Krishnamurti

Social constructs can be those of any group, including family, religion, education, business, etc. It's important to understand that all groups have some shared beliefs, whether conscious or not. Often, those shared beliefs include the unconscious assumption that social constructs should not be questioned. This leads us to not question our own thoughts and beliefs and thereby become fused with our mind, thinking it's who we are.

In Stage 3, we tend to believe and think mostly what is acceptable within our identity group and avoid or repress thoughts that are unacceptable. This gives us a model for certain ways of thinking and believing, but toward the end of Stage 3, we start breaking out of such structures, looking for new ways to understand ourselves and life.

Katherine: I learned the lingo and beliefs of my company to fit it. I even took on those beliefs as my own, which felt safe and acceptable, since that's what everyone in my team believed. I can see that I feel constrained by that, but I'm scared of being thrown out for thinking different.

- Journal about 3 things you believe that are important to you. They can be beliefs about anything.
- With each of those beliefs ask yourself "Am I open to this belief changing?" If the answer is no, journal about why.

Stage 3 – Emotions

Location Description: Only allowing feelings acceptable to identity group

Needs: To feel safe, loved, and know that we belong

"We all know that suppressing emotion can kill you both spiritually and physically." – Lisa Kleypas

In Stage 3, we learn about our emotions based on what is permissible by those around us. If those supporting our development have a positive relationship with their own emotions, we will acquire healthy emotional habits. If our supporters are themselves repressing their feelings, we are likely to pick up similar patterns.

It's here that we often suppress certain feelings or emphasize others in order to fit in and feel safe. While this helps us get the support we need to grow, avoiding the feelings we think are unsafe begins to disconnect us from all our emotions, which act as a sort of compass for how to live authentically. As we move toward the end of Stage 3, we become much more aware of our need to be authentic and break away from the impulse to conform.

Jane: I quickly learned which emotions weren't acceptable to those around me, so I tried to suppress them. This was actually incredibly painful and it made me really sad, another emotion that wasn't acceptable. So I eventually had to disconnect from my all emotions just to feel ok.

- Journal about any emotions you tend to avoid or suppress. Do you know why?
- Observe your emotions without judgment or trying to fix them or make them different.
- Express your true feelings with people you trust to keep your confidence.

Stage 3 – Body

Location Description: Physical development shaped by social norms

Needs: To develop physically within acceptable social values

"Your net worth to the world is usually determined by what remains after your bad habits are subtracted from your good ones." – Benjamin Franklin

As mammals, we learn how to be a physical body in the world by templating on how those around us use their bodies. This includes how we dress, what we eat, how we exercise, what activities we engage in, and all our behaviors. We cannot help but model ourselves after the good and bad habits of our parents, the society in which we are raised, and the culture around us.

On the positive side, we learn all kinds of very positive and healthy habits while we are being conditioned by parents and others. Gifts that our parents have are often communicated to children unconsciously. This process is so natural, that as adults we might not even notice how we gained many of our skills until we consciously connect them with our parents. On the negative side, the body can be deeply conditioned by patterns of tension, self-holding, self-abuse, constricted breathing, and limited awareness of physical needs, which we inherit unconsciously.

Kate: My mom taught me simplicity – minimal makeup and comfortable clothing not to be overdone. I was taught that the body was not something to give much attention to. This served me well in many ways, but later I realized I was pretty dissociated from my body and had to do a lot of work to reconnect with my physical self.

- Get regular physical exercise. Pay special attention to the balance between the need to find your own limits and your body's need not to be overly taxed.
- Journal about your relationship with what and how you eat. Are your conditioned patterns around food working for your body?

Stage 4: Rational Striving

Stage Overview: Drive to know, prove, succeed, achieve, or win

- Subjective: Driven to live logically, achieve worthiness and independence
- Observable: Observable independence-driven behavior
- Relational: Success or facts valued over connection
- Systemic: Interacting based on hierarchy, merit, and competence

Needs: To find self-esteem and self-reliance through accomplishment

Identity: I'm independent and improving myself

"If you want to fly, you have to give up what weights you down." – Anonymous

In Stage 3 we felt pressure to conform to the lifeways of those who were helping us develop. Stage 4 begins with feeling the urge to individuate, to free ourselves from any person or group that appears to limit us or tell us who we should be. While it's true that few of us really know who we are in Stage 3, we sense that to find ourselves, we must set boundaries with our previous influences and find our own authenticity. Stage 4 is about shifting from the need to conform to discovering who you are in your own right. For most, this is a difficult leap, because the earlier part of our life required us to conform in order to get our needs met. The need to understand who we are is so strong at this stage that one way or another, with or without loving support, it drives most to leave the nest (in some fashion), find our own wings, and fly free to discover ourselves and what we are here to be in this world.

In Stage 4, we discover the power of self-authoring, of choosing, taking responsibility for our choices, and learning about the consequences of our choices. Most are drawn to explore the concrete and material levels of life because, out of our primary need for physical survival, our attention has been focused more on the physical level of life.

Questions can arise such as "How can I make myself a better person?" or "How can I succeed and make my own way?" or "Do I need to sacrifice my deepest principles in order to survive on my own?" Here, we are driven to find answers.

Stage 4 is a time for gaining the life skills necessary to become independent. Here we value autonomy and self success (personally and professionally) over interdependence (with friends, family, or teams at work). That doesn't necessarily mean "successful" in the ways the world tends to define it; it means we learn to fend for ourselves as autonomous adults. The independence learned in this stage will later mature into interdependence as we learn to work and play cooperatively with others.

In Stage 4, there is an emphasis on the role of mind-based will, which is why we call this stage "rational striving." The focus here is still mostly on external reality and the Domains of Body and Mind. The need is to become developed enough and sufficiently grounded in physical reality to survive and mature. As we develop in Stage 4, we start to notice that focusing on material experiences doesn't necessarily fulfill our needs to experience meaning and purpose. Toward the end of Stage 4, we start to experience the limits of life fixated on superficial levels, and we start to yearn for something deeper.

Sue: My seeking became an obsession to feel successful. The more I felt I accomplished and achieved, the better I felt ... temporarily, until I hit a bump, triggering another urge to feel okay or successful. Eventually I saw that grasping for success was causing me to endlessly chasing my tail and I started to wonder if I'd ever be satiated with external achievements no matter how grand they became.

- Write down what success means to you. If you can define it, you can achieve it.
- Set goals for yourself. Longer term goals should be things that truly matter to you. Short term goals, including daily or weekly goals, should be small enough that they are easy to attain, giving you confidence that you can achieve your aims.
- Journal about how your patterns of "success" and "failure" feel and what you conclude about them.

Stage 4 – Consciousness

Location Description: Controlling awareness to achieve wants

Needs: To discover that consciousness can help me achieve

"Some of us think holding on makes us strong, but sometimes it is letting go." -- Herman Hesse

In Stage 4 there's often the desire to have an edge over others, with an underlying striving and competitive energy. There's often not only the desire to achieve but to win. For example, if expanding awareness is going to give you the winning edge, then that's what you will go after.

Peter: At this Stage, I thought that becoming enlightened would get me everything I wanted in life. I spent most of my time and money seeking enlightenment because I thought that would fix everything. Looking back on that, so much of that drive was based in my mental ideas and ideals.

- Meditate. Find a comfortable place without distractions and sit comfortably with your eyes closed for at least 15 minutes. Be aware of your own breath moving in and out. Allow thoughts to come and go. Allow a transition before returning to activity.
- During the day, practice noticing that you are aware of everything you experience.

Stage 4 – Uniqueness

Location Description: Using uniqueness to achieve wants

Needs: To discover my individuality while striving to achieve goals

"Success is not in what you have, but who you are."
– Bo Bennett

In Stage 4, we tend to compromise our uniqueness to achieve. This is often seen in work situations. We might compromise our personal uniqueness in order to be seen in a certain way by our boss, or to achieve a certain goal. It's usually not conscious, but later in Stage 4 we start to notice the negative impacts that hiding or compromising our beliefs, rhythms, preferences, strengths, etc. has on ourselves and those around us. Compromising our own uniqueness makes it challenging not only to appreciate our own uniqueness, but also that of others. As we recognize these impacts, we are moved to find our own authenticity.

Brooke: I took jobs I didn't really want, thinking they would help me climb the ladder. The problem was that my motivation, passion, and focus dissipated and left me drained. I finally realized that compromising my unique gifts, and playing parts that were not 'me', never actually served me.

- Journal about what you hide from others and why. In what ways does that work to your benefit? In what ways does that hurt you and others?
- Contemplate: See if you notice yourself judging others as weird. Explore the feelings that make you want to hold others as separate or less than you.
- List all the ways you are werid.

Stage 4 – Mind

Location Description: Trying to rationally optimize one's life

Needs: To be in control of my mind

"Knowledge comes, but wisdom lingers."
– Calvin Coolidge

Stage 4 is dominated by unconscious management of thinking. There's a belief that if I control my thoughts then I can control my life, or that by collecting knowledge, I can prove myself and get what I want. Mind-based rational striving is prevalent particularly in developed western cultures and businesses.

Rational striving is an important and necessary stage of mental development. We need to learn how to use our mind to help us navigate life and accomplish things. There are limits to how much control over mind is actually effective, but we don't usually notice them until we start feeling how this Stage is no longer working for us. To feel what's not working for us, it's important to value our emotions as much as our thoughts and beliefs.

Mary: I grew up being taught to change my thoughts in order to get the outcomes I wanted. I also tried to read every book, take every course, and go to every workshop in order to feel "I knew enough". In the end, I realized that no matter how many books I read or degrees I slaved over, the feeling of "not enough" was still there.

- During your day, pay attention to the endless flow of your thoughts. When thoughts flow in a direction that you know isn't good for you, practice putting your attention on something that helps you.
- Notice any tendencies you may have to prove to others that you know a lot. Without self-judgment, explore where that comes from. What fears are associated with this tendency?
- Watch the patterns of thoughts that consistently come into your mind. Notice the feelings that come along with the repeating thoughts.

Stage 4 – Emotions

Location Description: Minimizing emotions to avoid complexity and achieve goals

Needs: To feel okay outside my family and support systems

"What you hide controls you." – Anonymous

In Stage 4, we start learning to give ourselves permission to feel however we feel, despite how accepted we are by those around us. As you start following your own guidance, it becomes important to discover how to feel ok in yourself. Here we often experience an unconscious attempt to manage emotions in order to feel sufficient. Sometimes, the drive to know, prove, succeed, achieve, or win, can be used to distract from feelings of pain, confusion, and discomfort that are almost inevitable when going through this important transition.

Lucy: Strong emotions were not very accepted in my family. I learned to suppress and manage my feelings in an effort to feel good enough. In the end, I realized that attempting to manipulate my emotions never really worked. It was like holding my breath, but emotionally, I slowly numbed out.

- When an uncomfortable emotion arises, consciously stay with it. When you notice it, let yourself feel it, lean into it, and fully accept it.
- Talk about your emotional taboos with someone you can trust and ask them to help you be ok with those feelings.

Stage 4 – Body

Location Description: Ignoring or over-managing the body

Needs: To discover the body's limits

"I think there's so much emphasis on body image and results and outcomes, but really what you should be after is to be healthy and to feel good about yourself." – Abby Wambach

In Stage 4, most people are either under-emphasizing taking care of their physical body, ignoring their physical needs, or actively abusing their body for the sake of perfection, distraction from pain, or other reasons. Health issues are often not noticed or tended to. Some tend to overemphasize physical wellness to the detriment of their other Domains. Micromanaging is part of this; overly trying to control how the body functions or looks.

At this Stage, there is attachment to the belief that we'll fulfill our physical needs and desires by following a particular mental strategy. In actual practice, there is no set of mental strategies that will give us everything our bodies need for strength and wellness. But in Stage 4, we often use our mind to resist what we don't want and push for what we think we want using our will – even if our body disagrees.

There's also a tendency to try to control how we look to others in order to be accepted. It may take some time to notice that if people like the image we present, we never know if they actually like who we are, or if they just like the image we're projecting. Similarly, we might manipulate our body to achieve some ideal look or performance standard. Hopefully, sooner or later we'll notice when we cross the line into achieving at the expense of our own health.

On the positive side, when we are encouraged to push the limits of our physical capacities, it helps the body to grow and find out what it can achieve. It's actually extremely important for the body to go into this almost competitive driving phase so we can see what our bodies are capable of.

Lynn: Because I felt so imperfect, I micromanaged my body in the hope of feeling better. I became a fitness and nutrition expert, and followed very tight nutritional protocols and fitness regimes, all with the hope that I'd feel good and in control. In truth, that didn't work very well; I still feel uncomfortable about my body and I'm almost always overly concerned about how I'm being seen by others.

- Spend time consciously not doing things. Relax, be in nature, or hang out with friends, with nothing to do but enjoy.
- Stretch your body; consider yoga or other formal body disciplines. The aim is to feel what your body needs and wants, no matter what others believe is good or right.
- Before you do something to your body, ask your body what it wants. Love your body enough to consciously follow what it wants.

Stage 5: Equality Harmony

Stage Overview: Promoting "oneness" by battling hierarchical differences together

- Subjective: Valuing openness, diversity, and sameness
- Observable: Idealistically challenges conventional norms
- Relational: Prioritizing harmony and connection with others
- Systemic: Interacting in an egalitarian fashion

Needs: To experience universal connection with others and the planet

Identity: I'm part of humanity and the planet

"He who lives in harmony with himself lives in harmony with the universe." – Marcus Aurelius

Sooner or later, the drive toward achievement in Stage 4 yields to the recognition that attention to the exteriors and surfaces of life is not giving us deeper meaning, connection, or fulfillment. Stage 5 is characterized by a strong desire to go deeper, to discover things that are subtler, more connective, more meaningful, and more universal. People often explore a range of things like meditation, yoga, emotional intelligence practices, biofeedback technologies, New Age practices, crystals, subtle energy effects, channeling, and other experiences that take us beyond the surface.

In the Location Description "Promoting 'oneness' by battling hierarchical differences together," oneness is in quotes because in Stage 5, this is more an idea or feeling than a realization of underlying unity. The sense of battling hierarchy is part of a desire for equality and harmony; we don't yet see how hierarchies and peer relationships have their place and can co-exist and be of mutual benefit.

Stage 5 can bring an idealistic urge to help others or save the world. This is a good thing, yet much of that energy turns out to be for our own healing, at least at this point. The desire for feelings of equality and harmony can often be a counterbalance to feelings of being controlled by authorities or feelings of deep disharmony, which can be difficult to cope with.

Lisa: In work meetings, we would go round and round on discussions in hopes to get consensus before moving forward. This was exhausting, and cost our teams and the company a tremendous amount of time and resources.

Bill: I saw no need for hierarchy, and I wanted consensus on everything before moving forward. Making money and "being worldly" became unimportant relative to my mission to help people. I just wanted everyone to get along and live in peace.

- Journal about what harmony in relationships means to you and why you seek it.
- Journal about why you resist thoughts and feelings you don't like.
- Find a beautiful place in nature. Notice the harmony that pervades, despite the obvious coexistence of life and death.

Stage 5 – Consciousness

Location Description: Seeking universal connection and learning to witness experience

Needs: To connect with our deeper self and learn self-transcendence through witnessing

"We are the witness through which the universe becomes conscious of its magnificence." – Anonymous

In Stage 5, we start to get that there's more to life than what we perceive on the surface. We start reaching for a bigger sense of self, including the limitless aspect of life.

We might find ourselves starting to become curious about what consciousness is because it might make us more peaceful or might show us what's equal between all beings, which it actually does. At this point, consciousness might be felt more strongly, sometimes with the sense of witnessing experience. Subjectively, we can begin to notice that all experiences – no matter what the content – are fundamentally different from the part of us that registers experience.

Roger: I was sitting in meditation and found myself completely absorbed in absolute nothingness, yet I was clearly awake. There were no thoughts, just existence without limit. After about 15 minutes, I came out of that state and opened my eyes. The feeling of infinite awareness lasted about 24 hours, and became my first recognition of the part of me that was witnessing my own experience. There was a new ability to witness all of what was happening, rather than merely being absorbed in it.

- Sit in meditation with your eyes closed and watch your thoughts and sensations without any attempt to control what you experience. Practice noticing that you are witnessing your own thoughts and sensations.
- Practice gazing with a partner. Sit together silently, holding each other's gaze. Relax and simply witness the parade of thoughts, sensations, and perceptions that spontaneously occur. After an agreed time, thank each other and discuss your experience of noticing the witness consciousness or being it. Also notice and discuss what sensations or perceptions tend to pull you out of knowing that you are the witness.

Stage 5 – Uniqueness

Location Description: Valuing uniqueness to promote egalitarian ideals

Needs: To find harmony with others in the midst of unique differences

"One of the greatest regrets in life is being what others would want you to be, rather than being yourself." – Shannon L. Alder

At Stage 5, most people control or manipulate their uniqueness to promote feelings of equality, peace, love, or harmony. The unconscious battle against hierarchy and differences also ends up keeping our own uniqueness in check, which becomes self-destructive.

In this Stage, there's a tendency to stifle our impulses to confront things that will create waves, difficulties, or frictions from a desire to avoid feeling disharmony. The reason we call it equality/harmony is because there's a tendency to avoid the tension between people with more power and resources and people with less power and resources by imposing ideas and actions that emphasize sameness.

Stephanie: Depending on where I was or who I was with, I would blend in to avoid disharmony. I had lots of friends, but I finally noticed that I'd lost track of what makes me uniquely me. Eventually it became obvious that being myself was more important than avoiding friction with others.

- Journal about the ways you are unique. Write down at least 10 ways you show up uniquely. Then write about the gifts that come with your uniqueness.
- Contemplate what stops you from simply expressing your unique self. Is there something you don't want to feel? What does your mind tell you might happen if you do express yourself?

Stage 5 – Mind

Location Description: Seeking peace of mind through positive thinking

Needs: To recognize the fruitlessness of manipulating "negative" thoughts with "positive" ones

"Peace is the result of retraining your mind to process life as it is, rather than as you think it should be." –Wayne W. Dyer

It becomes apparent in Stage 5 that much of our thinking is negative in the sense that it's about reacting to or fighting with ourselves and reality because we don't like our experience. So, we naturally want to find more positive ways of thinking. Positive psychology can be useful because it helps give a more balanced view by counteracting our survival-based "negativity bias." However, if taken to an extreme (which some schools of positive psychology can do), we can think we should eliminate all negative thoughts, which turns into fighting with self, a battle that can never bring peace of mind.

In Stage 5, the urge toward equality can be mistakenly interpreted to mean that everyone's ideas are equally useful in all situations, which is clearly not true. For example, when designing a new rocket engine, the opinions of the engineers are much more valuable to the enterprise than the ideas of someone who knows nothing about rocket science. What's actually needed at this Stage is recognition that all beings have equal value. Someone who is great at designing a rocket engine is no more valuable than the massage therapist who helps the engineer find ease in their body after a long day's work.

The Stage 5 capacity to start seeing our own inner workings bring us the capacity to notice the endless ways our mind tries to make meaning or create judgment out of every observation. You start to see this in the moment, along with the many ways that believing all such concepts can lead us astray. Seeing this, we start becoming free from relating with our mind as if it was in total control.

Megan: Whenever a negative thought would appear, I would try to exchange it for what I thought was a better, more positive thought, believing these mental gymnastics would create a better experience. When actually, it was nothing more than rearranging the chairs on the Titanic. I realized that creating a new thought in hope of cancelling out the previous one is actually exhausting, and it didn't stop me from having negative thoughts anyway.

- Journal – What do I get from trying to change my thoughts?
- Practice discriminating your thoughts from your feelings. Notice that some feelings can drive certain thought patterns. When this happens, see if you can process your feelings on their own level instead of trying to work them out in your mind.

Stage 5 – Emotions

Location Description: Prioritizing love and positivity over disharmony

Needs: To feel harmonious and a sense of equal value among humans

"Unexpressed emotions will never die. They are buried alive and will come forth later in uglier ways." – Sigmund Freud

Stage 5 can be seen as a response to the concrete, materially-oriented values of Stage 4. Having experienced enough of self-authoring and independence, we start wanting to experience more meaningful connections with others and the planet. We want to find universal love and experience subtler, deeper phenomena.

A common detour here is to think we can heal ourselves of negative emotional states by acting happy or replacing them with positive feelings. It's good that we try new things to break up our conditioned behaviors, yet it's easy to get stuck trying to manipulate ourselves into preferable emotional states. Trying to make everything look and feel positive to yourself or others is a way of superimposing our preferences on what's actually happening. This turns out to be another form of war with life. It also disconnects us from the importance of uncomfortable feelings. If we only listen to half of what life is trying to bring us, we're missing a lot.

JJ: For a long time, I practiced replacing my bad feelings with positive ones. I would cover my "negative" feelings by declaring a sense of love and gratitude, like putting whipped cream on a pile of moldy food, hoping I'd only taste the whipped cream.

- Try not fixing or changing your emotions. See what happens if you are simply present with them.
- Our ability to love others is limited to our ability to love ourselves. As you move through your day, practice loving who you are and everything you do. This doesn't mean you will like everything you feel or experience; it's simply a practice of self-acceptance and self-embrace.

Stage 5 – Body

Location Description: Seeking harmony through physical disciplines

Needs: To find physical harmony

"Don't let your mind bully your body."– Anonymous

It's common in Stage 5 to seek harmony by purifying the body. This is a good thing, because an appropriate amount of that improves health, and can help us relax and settle into all Domains, not just our body. This can become unhealthy when our ideas about what's good for our body override what our body truly wants and needs.

An important challenge is to find harmony or okay-ness with physical body experiences that we don't like; otherwise, if we're always trying to fix our body, it's just another form of battling with ourselves.

Jessica: For years I practiced hot yoga, dietary cleanses, and silent retreats... all in an attempt to detox my system and experience more harmony and connection with myself. Those things helped for sure, but each time, I got used to my new state and found that I always wanted more. I kept assuming there was something wrong with me that I could fix by being more purified.

- Sit or lie down with eyes closed and scan your body from head to toes, relaxing with every breath. Feel whatever is present without judgment.
- See if you can identify physical sensations you have been interpreting as bad or wrong. Then just be with those sensations, without trying to change them.

Stage 6: Inclusive

Stage Overview: Identities crumble, creating flexibility, depth, and the capacity to integrate whole being

- Subjective: Including as much of self, others, and life as possible
- Observable: Seeking deeply meaningful experiences
- Relational: Including deeper differences in connections
- Systemic: Flexibly adapting to roles in different contexts

Needs: To release limiting beliefs about self, others, and world

Identity: I'm deepening and including

"When you begin to awaken layers will be shed. You may experience rage, depression, anxiety, fear. Ride the wave, allow these things to exit your system because your limited sense of self is being shed so that your deeper self can emerge. Embrace the transition." – Anonymous

Sooner or later, we begin to discover how infinitely huge the world is and how small our awareness of it has been. This extends to our awareness of how huge we are ourselves, and how small our sense of self has been. In Stage 6 the desire to go beyond all limits, both concrete and subtle, becomes increasingly powerful. We realize that we must become radically inclusive of all life experiences, especially ourselves just as we are, even the parts we don't like.

For many, embracing what is uncomfortable can be a difficult proposition. If you've spent most of your life actively doing, fixing, and improving, why simply accept yourself as you are, when you could be so much better? The answer is simple: because you cannot drop into, fully realize, and become yourself if you're too busy trying to fix and avoid what you don't like about yourself.

In order for us to actually be more inclusive in our awareness of self, others, and world, our previously limited sense of self must decay. The decay process is often experienced as an unwilled dropping of ideals. After all the work and striving in Stages 4 and 5, Stage 6 can often bring a feeling of failure to achieve our greatest aspirations. You may find yourself uncharacteristically shying away from those whose lives are still about the great ascent to the peak of success or attainment, however they define that.

No matter what our aspirations have been, we must find a way to shift from our previous mental ways of orienting our entire lives. To be in tune with our whole self, we must decay out of exclusively mind-based strategies and learn to value depth, truth, honesty, feelings, and reality. We must learn to embrace the unique truth of our entire being in each and every moment. We must learn to make decisions from our whole being, not just our head.

As we allow ourselves to drop out of exclusive identification with our thoughts and ideas, we encounter parts of ourselves we're rather not see. We notice our own limits and conditioning, and we see all the ways we've distracted ourselves from discomfort by putting glitter and smiley-face stickers on the inside of our own mental prison walls. But have courage; seeing such patterns is the beginning of a process that will bring much deeeper freedom and authenticity.

"No matter how difficult and painful it may be, nothing sounds as good to the soul as the truth". – Martha Beck

Stage 6 brings a strong need to honor our own truth, whether we like it or not. Sometimes that's not so hard, and sometimes that's very challenging. But at this stage of your life, following your truth is what matters, even if that leads you toward feelings or recognitions you've been avoiding. Here we start to realize that we could never truly live in integrity if we keep avoiding what we don't like in ourselves.

Turning toward the despair hiding in our own depths can feel like a "dark night of the soul." If we are hurting, feeling lost, or feeling disconnected from others and from our deepest source, why should we turn toward that pain? Isn't that the wrong direction? For most, learning to embrace pain is the opposite of what we've been taught. Such conditioning makes the practice of radical embrace all the more challenging, yet also rewarding. The good news is that welcoming your current, in-the-moment truth brings you home to yourself and frees up tremendous energy that was previously absorbed in unconscious fixing and resistance. This relaxes and deepens us, increases our patience and contentment with life, and creates the foundation for realization of boundlessness in Stage 7.

Stage 6 brings the willingness to explore our conditioning and discover patterns that have been unconsciously running us, usually for many years and often decades. This exploration is deeply important in order to release energy and attention that was bound up in self-limiting and self-negating patterns in every Domain and View of our being. Some resolve to confront their own conditioning with the energy of a warrior who will not be stopped. Others feel dragged into it, all the while knowing they have become too conscious of their own reality to be able to continue hiding from their own darkness. Either way, as we start to penetrate our conditioning, we are shown what needs healing or upgrading and we are constantly challenged in our willingness to stay fully present with it. But as we become more and more deeply present with the truth of who we are, both light and dark, we begin to understand that we are far more perfect than we could have imagined, while simultaneously being very flawed.

The more we are willing to cooperate with the ups and downs of life, the more we are present with what's actually happening. This increasing capacity for presence makes us aware of more subtle and connective layers of life. This brings an increased capacity to embrace complexity, paradox, and fuzzy lines, and allows us to be more aware of everything happening around us and within greater contexts. We start to notice that all stages of development are perfect; we don't need to judge or fix them. Here we learn to truly embrace the whole spectrum of life, knowing that everything is exactly as it should be, including the endless desire for more and better. Embracing experiences that we previously rejected liberates the energy we were using to negate those experiences and helps us notice that facing into life is more rewarding than avoiding and resisting the parts we don't like.

Ella: I questioned who I was... Am I consciousness? My body? How do I reconcile feeling I'm actually all of it? Parts of who I thought I was were crumbling away, creating a lot of fear as well as a lot of freedom. Simultaneously I wanted to express all aspects of me at the same time, integrating everything and neglecting nothing. I started to welcome back parts of me I pushed away. Relationally, I started to value and love other's opinions, perspectives, and experiences. I was able to see the truth and power in all opposites – polarities like right and wrong, good and bad, etc. disappeared, and discovering the truth in all angles and views became interesting – there was room for it all.

- Explore your relationship with discomfort in all Domains. Go into your day looking for ways you feel uncomfortable and notice what you tend to do when you feel that. Practice just feeling and embracing your discomforts.
- Is there a feeling you've been trying to fix, perhaps for your whole life? Something you are sure is wrong, something you think if you fix, then you'll be happy? Find that feeling and embrace it. Know that it's not wrong, it's an essential part of who you are. Embrace that feeling not to make it go away, but to come home to yourself.

- Welcome all of yourself and your responses, no matter how conditioned they are. Welcoming practice has three parts: 1) Recognize some aspect of yourself that you've been fixing, avoiding, or pushing away, 2) give it permission to be exactly as it is, and 3) embrace it. Practice this several times a day, and you'll start to experience more free energy and ok-ness in yourself.
- In addition to welcoming things that are challenging, it's important to embrace and engage with things you enjoy that feel good and nourishing.

Stage 6 – Consciousness

Location Description: Expanding awareness starts dissolving limited sense of self

Needs: To allow previous senses of self to fall away

"The key to growth is the introduction of higher dimensions of consciousness into our awareness."– Lao Tzu

The expansion of consciousness in Stage 6 begins to illuminate our limited sense of self. Previous self-sense constructions begin to crumble, sometimes causing challenging internal shifts. Yet, these changes make it increasingly obvious that who and what we are is far bigger than we thought. Discovering a bigger, more inclusive sense of self creates a whole new foundation of flexibility and openness.

At Stage 6, the desire to expand our sense of self pushes us beyond further mental constructions about who we are and what we can accomplish. Attempts to make ourselves better by visualizing, setting goals, and practicing mental techniques fall short because our basic motivation is to go deeper, to find ultimate answers about life and self. Through meditation, contemplation, and consciousness practices, we can find those ultimate answers.

Pam: After doing some consciousness exercises, I started to notice aspects of who I thought I was disappear. There was a dissolving of identities in a way that was quite freeing, but also uncomfortable because I'd built my whole life on those identities. I didn't know how to handle the loss of those constructs, yet there was also a greater sense of openness, an ability to see and take in more without getting caught in my own thoughts, emotions, and reactions.

- Sit with eyes closed in meditation on simple presence. Allow thoughts to move through you without resistance. Once you feel simple presence, notice anything that seems to remove you from that.
- Practice allowing thoughts and feelings while simultaneously being the presence. Notice that this presence is witnessing your thoughts, sensations, and emotions.

- Be persistent in trying different approaches. Each person much find their own way to discover their own infinite nature.

Stage 6 – Uniqueness

Location Description: Starting to accept who one is and is not

Needs: To let go of "who I should be" and relax into "who I am"

"Waking up to who you are requires letting go of who you imagine yourself to be." – Alan Watts

At Stage 6, our idealism about who we thought we should be starts to decay. We might find ourselves losing past beliefs or switching paths – or even friends – to be more authentic. At this point, it becomes obviously painful to go against our own natural tendencies. We find ourselves willing to push the envelope and question some basic assumptions we previously took for granted.

We are no longer attached to the approval and love of

others to the point of compromising our uniqueness. There's a willingness to begin standing for our unique truth, even if we lose the love of others. We start to see that being our true self brings us friends and supporters who love and value who we truly are. The willingness to be uncomfortable gives us the capacity to step into and own our uniqueness as never before.

This process of decaying out of the belief that you can be someone you're not is necessary in order to become who you actually are. This process of decay can be challenging; it can feel like "existential capsizing" because in many ways, your whole life is turning upside down.

Part of what happens in Stage 6 is that we learn to stop being at war with who we are and own our unique truth. If someone says "you're a weirdo", a person in Stage 6 might reply "You're right, I am a weirdo." At this point we can do that, because being who we are has become much more important than conforming to anyone's expectations, including our own. What really matters at this point is to truly love and accept ourselves for who we actually are, versus who we thought we should be.

Karen: I finally started to acknowledge and allow all my hidden parts to show up; the good, the bad, and the ugly. I was learning to love all aspects of who I was, even if they were unpopular, made no sense, or contradicted one another.

- Contemplate and journal about the challenges that come with being your unique self. What do you feel makes it hard or even dangerous for you to be completely true to yourself?
- Notice any ways in which you deny your truth in relationships. Do you prematurely agree with others? How does it feel when you do that?

Stage 6 – Mind

Location Description: Limiting beliefs about self and life begin disintegrating

Needs: To allow and include all beliefs, including conflicting ones

"Over time, we amass limiting beliefs about how life supposedly is – beliefs that are not valid. Then we allow these limiting beliefs to stop us from fully living our happiest lives."
– Karen Salmansohn

At Stage 6, our attachments to beliefs that no longer align with our reality begin to fall away. Yet, we can also see that all of our beliefs – and those of others – are perfect in their own way. At Stage 6, we are moved to practice embracing all forms of thought as points of view, rather than seeing beliefs as right or wrong. Here we adopt a larger perspective that creates much more flexibility, openness, and capacity to value other's views. This inclusive disposition proves to be much more relaxing compared with defending thoughts and beliefs as if our lives depended on them. It's still true that some beliefs are very important to us, but those turn out to be few and far between, relative to the volume of thoughts we experience every day.

At this point in our development, we start to recognize our inner committee. Some parts of ourselves want something, other parts want completely opposite things. Instead of trying to resolve this apparent disharmony, we notice that the real disharmony is our resistance to this fact of how our mind operates. We begin to accept ourselves with all our paradoxes and polarities intact. We begin to see that we can hold opposites without reacting or taking sides. We can start to see how opposites integrate and work together. We learn to love and accept ourselves, despite being both dark and light.

What empowers this more expansive relationship with our mind is our newly emerging capacity to become less exclusively identified with our mind. We start to notice how much we've been lost in and identified with our mind. It's as if we've had our head in a TV for our whole life, and suddenly someone shakes us, saying "that's just a TV. Come back to the rest of you."

Mike: I was so in my head and cut off from my feelings. If someone disagreed with me, I had to defend myself because I thought I was my ideas. But then I started to see that I'm much bigger than my mind. Over time, I noticed that I didn't have to be right all the time; it was ok for my mind to be limited. I could see my mind as just a part of myself that's trying to help me.

- Practice observing your thoughts as if they were things said on TV. Not everything that's said on TV is important, and not every every thought in your mind is worth attaching yourself to.
- Question and challenge your own thoughts and beliefs and be willing to change your perspectives.
- Listen to the opinions of people who have very different beliefs than yours. Notice how you feel, and whether you're willing to fully feel it or not. Try on beliefs that conflict with your own and see what happens if you're just curious and don't take sides.

Stage 6 – Emotions

Location Description: Learning to stay present to all emotions

Needs: To be present with feelings of dissolution while opening to the larger truth of my experience

"Feelings or emotions are the universal language and are to be honored. They are the authentic expression of who you are at your deepest place." –Judith Wright

In Stage 6, we become more embracing of all feelings in our emotional spectrum. Patterns of avoiding and reacting to feelings we dislike begin to thaw, a process that spans many Stages before we find ourselves living in deep emotional fluidity.

The increased willingness to allow old identities to crumble while feeling whatever is present allows our heart to open as never before. This passage can be extremely challenging, especially if you've been conditioned to think that feeling emotional or vulnerable is wrong, bad, or weak. In any case, what drives this increasing willingness and desire to feel is the recognition that there is no point in trying to escape your own truth. At this stage it's obvious that grasping for what we want and avoiding what we don't want actually makes our lives worse. That was a lot of pushing and pulling that occupied our attention in the past, but at Stage 6, we no longer have the motivation – or the energy – to be constantly manipulating our experience. We are forced to just be with our experience, like it or not.

The willingness to feel what is uncomfortable allows us to discriminate between necessary and unnecessary pain. We begin to notice that some pain is necessary, and we learn to accept that. We also see conditioned patterns of resistance in ourselves that have tended to cause unnecessary pain. One of those patterns is the tendency to react and create drama around necessary pain. By more deeply accepting what is, we start to reduce the unnecessary pain of avoiding necessary pain.

The need to feel what is present also brings our attention to the many ways we've avoided our emotions in the hope of avoiding pain. The problem is, pain and pleasure are two sides of the same coin. If we don't feel our pain, we can't fully feel pleasure or happiness. In Stage 6, we decay out of avoidance and start to feel everything.

If previously we thought that our emotions made us weak, at this point, we start to recognize that true strength is not about acting powerful; it's about finding the courage to remain centered in/as the stillness with any emotion that arises. This is what gives us the power to connect with our deeper selves, others, and stay present and open in most any situation.

Brenda: I cried a lot. I was releasing a lot. I felt like an iceberg thawing out. Emotions were flooding my system, arising in waves. I finally just let it happen. I was finally feeling everything – I was starting to fully feel all of life for the first time. My ability to connect with others became much deeper and way more fulfilling. And my empathy for others went way up.

- When you find yourself getting triggered or reacting to a situation, take a moment and name the emotion. Then simply feel it and embrace it, as deeply as you can, without blaming yourself or others, and without trying to fix it or understand it. Practice sinking into the emotions without distracting yourself from them.
- Next time you put on a happy face, ask yourself if that's what you're really feeling.
- Practice speaking the truth of what you feel in your relationships. Be careful not to blame others, simply take responsibility for your own feelings. The more skillfully you can do this, the more others will feel your integrity.

Stage 6 - Body

Location Description: Noticing unaligned physical conditioning

Needs: To allow the release of physical and energetic constrictions; beginning attunement to body needs, ability to see your own body patterns, how your body responds uniquely to food, exercise, and all experience.

"We humans have lost the wisdom of genuinely resting and
relaxing. We worry too much. We don't allow our bodies to
heal, and we don't allow our minds and hearts to heal."
– Thich Nhat Hanh

As early forms of identity begin to crumble, it's natural to ask ourselves questions like "Is this behavior natural for me, or is it just my conditioning?" The deeper this inquiry goes, the more it frees up our bodies, so we naturally begin to move in deeper harmony with our unique physical nature. Old patterns and ways of moving our body that were conditioned in earlier stages (including how we eat, how we dress, and how we behave in different situations) begin to dissolve. Having these patterns start to dissolve can be both frightening and rejuvenating. It's scary because we don't know who we are without our conditioned patterns, and losing our previous sense of self can feel threatening. But finding the faith to step into that investigation frees up tremendous energy because the more we move in ways that are natural to our specific uniqueness, the more happy, free, and energetic we feel.

Rob: My wife gave me feedback that whenever I said something challenging to her, I would flinch. I tracked it down to my childhood. When I'd say something that challenged my mom, she'd hit me. It took me some time to become fully aware of this and allow that defense system to relax.

- Explore your physical patterns, looking for those that feel out of harmony with who you are.
- When letting go of old conditioning, it's important to be held by others so we can feel safe to let go of old patterns. Find a trusted friend, loved one, or ally who can physically hold you while you unwind.
- Give yourself the gift of a massage or some other therapy that helps you completely relax.
- Find healing through your connection with nature.

Stage 7: Awakening

Stage Overview: Fundamental shifts and openings into boundlessness

- Subjective: Recognizing self as boundless
- Observable: Observable wonder, clarity, compassion and fascination with the world
- Relational: Learning to relate from the transpersonal
- Systemic: Beginning of co-creative flow

Needs: To recognize boundlessness in all Domains

Identity: I am boundlessness

"What lies behind you and what lies in front of you, pales in comparison to what lies inside of you."
– Ralph Waldo Emerson

At Stage 7 we cannot ignore the urge to find the transcendent truths of life and self. We yearn for something deeper than the limits of our human lives. Here we seek direct experience of that which goes beyond our thoughts, emotions, and senses.

Awakening is an endless process, but we call this Stage "Awakening" because the subjective experience brings experiences of infinite presence or spaciousness, which can appear in any Domain. These experiences bring an enormous shift in the sense of self. We realize that spaciousness is the core of who we are. Another way to say this is that consciousness awakens to itself within all Domains.

For some, the shift from assuming we were just this limited human person to knowing ourselves as fundamentally limitless is sudden and radical. For these people, the experience can be simultaneously liberating and disorienting. Others experience the shift into boundlessness in a more gradual way that feels more ordinary. In any case, as we mature in Stage 7, the realization of boundlessness penetrates all Domains and informs them with the wisdom of infinity.

For some, the realization of boundless presence becomes instantly stable such that, from that moment on, the person is never in doubt about being the infinite, immortal, imperishable presence. This becomes the new context, no matter what experiences come and go. For others, this realization starts with a series of experiences of boundlessness, following a long series of oscillations before the presence of spaciousness can be fully realized and owned. In every case, the shift into this knowingness brings a form of deep peace and inner stability that cannot be found in material experience alone.

In our experience, most people experience boundlessness before the realization of infinity is fully stable. However, we encourage those we work with to deeply recognize the infinite end of the spectrum of being and to identify with and as it. This sets us up for a clear integration process in Stage 8 in which we know both the infinite and finite ends of our own spectrum, and can fully contemplate both together. The more grounded we are in awakened presence, the more directly we can integrate our human Domains in Stage 8.

Some refer to this stage as "post-conventional", because at this point you're not operating according to either your own conventions or society's. Because you start to see through your own and others' conditioned biases, you can make new decisions that take you in directions more aligned with your personal purpose.

External confirmation of experiences of boundlessness is important to help ground and claim the reality of it. We are so used to identifying ourselves as merely limited that when our identity shifts to our own transcendent nature, it can be easy to dismiss as unreal simply because it's non-material in nature. Having the experience of transcendence seen by another can help us recognize and claim this truth of our being.

Hannah: I had a major shift into the realization of my true nature, but for years it seemed elusive until I spoke with a teacher about it. Having that shift recognized by another made it much easier to recognize that for myself. From that point on, knowing my infinite nature never went away.

- Meditate on the question "Who am I?" It's important to understand that this question is not to evoke a mental response; it's to help you explore your sense of self.
- Start your day looking for the feeling of simple presence in ordinary experience. Notice what makes you think that's not there.

Stage 7 - Consciousness

Location Description: Awareness awakens as itself

Needs: To discover the infinite nature of one's subjectivity

"You are the sky. Everything else is just the weather."
— Pema Chödrön

In Stage 7, consciousness awakens as itself. We realize that for our entire previous life, we've been exclusively identified with our limited personal human self, which is now seen as only part of our total identity.

To say the least, this is a huge realization, and a complete shift in perspective. Toward the end of his life, Maslow called it self-transcendence, and put that at the top of his developmental hierarchy. For some people, it's a sudden realization that who they really are is imperishable, immortal, infinite beyond all space and time. This realization brings a sense of freedom and spacious perspective that goes beyond anything we've previously experienced.

The awakening of consciousness is experienced in many different ways according to our unique nature and conditioning. Some feel the presence of consciousness as if it were an external presence, entity, or person. Others experience consciousness as vast emptiness, boundless fullness, or the velvet blackness of the night sky. In all cases, the common element is a pervading awareness of limitlessness.

In our experience, the Stage 7 consciousness awakening is not complete until boundless presence is clearly recognized and persistent – and is known as your own essential nature. At some point, you learn to recognize it as yourself, not as something outside yourself. When you can claim that the boundlessness you experience is your own self, your consciousness has awakened in a fundamental way.

For some, that realization never goes away; for others, it comes and goes for some time. For these people, that recognition is deeply tested through oscillations in Stage 8 that challenge one to recognize the simultaneity of consciousness and all other Domains. But once it is known without a doubt that consciousness cannot be overshadowed, the stabile realization of consciousness can land simultaneous with the realization of unity in Stage 9.

At this stage there is a risk of what's called "spiritual bypassing," the tendency to place more attention or value on consciousness above the personal Domains (Uniqueness, Emotions, Mind, and Body). It's easy to see why that would be a preference; the experience of consciousness in its own right can be quite blissful. While it's important to experience and own the truth of that level of our being, avoiding the needs of our heart, body, or soul actually slows our whole being awakening process.

Regarding the recognition of "no self", some experience that as early as Stage 7, others as late as Stage 13. In any case, it's important to explore any degree to which selflessness may be masking a difficulty in embodying our human self, our personal domains. It's important not to bypass our humanness in an attempt to gain transcendence. We can never realize our total self without knowing we are both.

Please note that the reason we place the awakening of consciousness in the Dual Phase is because that realization is not yet unified with the other Domains. No matter how vast the awakening in Stage 7, it will become much larger, as we recognize in Stage 9 that infinite and finite are one.

Ron: I was doing a breathing exercise and after some time I realized that something was breathing me, and I began crying. Suddenly, I was awake as consciousness, and everything, including my own mind, was in front of ME. To this was a cosmic realization. I knew myself to be the one universal awareness. From that moment on, I experienced major shifts in every part of my life.

- Close your eyes and feel your face and your whole body. Then imagine picking up a magic eraser and use it to erase your face and your body. What remains? Explore if that feels like it's you.
- With eyes closed, feel yourself sitting at the back of your head, witnessing your thoughts and experiences as if from a distance.
- Once you can easily notice the sense of witnessing with your eyes closed, practice noticing the same sense of boundlessness with your eyes open.

Stage 7 - Uniqueness

Location Description: Realizing and appreciating one's uniqueness

Needs: To recognize and claim the inherent goodness and rightness of one's own unique gifts and limits

"Be yourself; everyone else is already taken." – Oscar Wilde

At this point in our development, we discover an unwillingness to stifle our uniqueness for anything, including love, approval, or appreciation. We start to fully love ourselves and the uniqueness we bring to life. We discover the capacity to connect with ourselves in a way that allows our uniqueness to come forward and blossom without being inhibited by fears of losing something external. After all, what good can it do to gain external things or experiences if we lose our authentic self in the process? Self abandonment never feels good.

This is the point at which we start realizing the incredibly deep beauty and value of not just our own, but everyone's uniqueness. We see everyone's uniqueness, as well as our own, plays a perfect part in the dance of life.

Grace: I worked for over 15 years at a job that just wasn't me. It paid well and made me feel important, but a part of me felt betrayed every day I went there. One day, I realized it was over; I couldn't do that anymore. I made a huge career switch, and now I finally feel aligned with myself.

- Write down what is good about each of your gifts and your limits.
- Reflect on and write down what is perfect about someone you don't like.

Stage 7 - Mind

Location Description: Able to witness thoughts while knowing oneself as the container of spaciousness

Needs: To release primary identification with mind and become conscious of thoughts and thought patterns.

*"To realize that you are not your thoughts is when
you begin to awaken." – Eckhart Tolle*

In Stage 7, there's an experience of spacious knowingness that discovers itself to be the container of all thoughts and beliefs. Some refer to this as "construct aware" because we become aware of the constructs created in our own mind. Identifying our sense of self with spaciousness allows us to be much less attached to our thoughts. We can see that some thoughts are helpful and practical, and others are part of conditioned patterns, many of which are self-destructive. This frees us to choose which thoughts – if any – to pursue, instead of being unconsciously led by our conditioned mental patterns.

At this point, we can more clearly see our own duality-based perspective than we've previously been able to. Consciousness appears as one reality, and thoughts appear as another. This duality can be perpelxing, but through the oscillations in Stage 8, we will eventually come to recognize that mind and consciousness are not separate.

Rob: When my sense of self shifted from my mind to my consciousness, all the activity of my thoughts was as if on a movie screen in front on me, and I felt myself as untouched by them.

- With eyes closed, notice that you are witnessing your thoughts. Notice that consciousness is the empty spaciousness through which your thoughts are passing. For some, it's easier to notice that no matter what attention is currently directed at, there's always space left over around the edges. Or something intangible that persists unchanged no matter what we experience.
- When you're good at noticing you are witnessing thoughts with your eyes closed, try maintaining that disposition with your eyes open, through all experience, physical, emotional, mental, visual, etc.

Stage 7 - Emotions

Location Description: Universal love is the space for all emotions

Needs: To love yourself deeply; to experience universal love

"You can search throughout the entire universe for someone who is more deserving of your love and affection than you are yourself, and that person is not to be found anywhere. You, yourself, as much as anybody in the entire universe, deserve your love and affection." – Buddha

The heart awakening is quite different from the Stage 7 awakening in other Domains. As suggested by the beautiful quote from the Buddha, this awakening often starts with realizing that despite your flaws, you truly deserve – and need – to love yourself completely. As you learn to love yourself, you will notice your love for others increasing. At some point, you may experience your heart bursting open for everyone and everything.

In the anecdote below, the distinction between universal love and personal love was an experience Sophie had to sift through for quite a while. Clearly, she was not personally in love with the garbage man, the person crossing the street, or the street signs; she was just experiencing intimate connection with everything and everyone. It took her some time to discriminate between the universal love and the personal emotions while allowing both to be present. Her initial heart awakening took time to stabilize because for a while it appeared to come and go (more on that in Stage 8). Eventually, she realized that universal love is larger than all personal emotions and is always present.

Some experience this in more subtle ways, perhaps as a warm embrace of self and others that never goes away, even when we dislike or disapprove of others. But one way or another, Stage 7 brings the awakening of transpersonal love. It brings a depth of the universal into our personal emotional realm and opens us to others in ways that weren't possible before. Knowing universal love makes it clear that this part of ourselves cannot be perturbed by anything we're feeling. On the foundation of this knowingness, we feel more deeply anchored amidst the ups and downs of life. We can allow all emotions to come and go... and discover a new freedom to feel and embrace our reality in the moment.

Sophie: I was in the grocery store and had a massive spontaneous heart awakening. I was looking around the store feeling in love with every single person. Everything I could see I was absolutely madly in love with and I couldn't figure out what was going on. I left the grocery store and started wandering around town and was looking around having this experience with everybody: the garbage man, the guy on the corner, the woman crossing the street. And it wasn't just with people; I was also feeling it was street signs and everything. It was an incredible opening of universal love and I was curious when this was going to fade. But it never fully faded. There was some oscillation, but this awakening eventually stabilized for me.

- Be present with someone who is sharing their feelings with you. Allow yourself to feel their joy and pain without trying to change any of it. Notice the sense of universal connection this creates.
- Notice the ways you've been conditioned to hate yourself. Journal about this and the impact it's had on your happiness.
- Find something you've been beating yourself up for and take a more compassionate look at yourself. Can you see that you did your best at the time?

Stage 7 - Body

Location Description: Experiencing spaciousness in the body

Needs: To realize that body exists within spacious emptiness

"Consciousness goes beyond the bounds of your body."
– Lily Cole

In this Stage, the apparent solidity of physical objects comes into question because we have the direct experience of spacious emptiness as the essence of our body. Also, the appearance of duality between body and consciousness becomes striking. On one hand, there is our physical body, and on the other, there is infinite nothingness, which feels like the opposite of physical reality. In Stage 7, our sense of self becomes rooted in nothingness, making us wonder how to relate with our body. This resolves as we awaken to unity in Stage 9 and realize that body and consciousness are different appearances of the same thing.

The realization that infinity is the essence of our body is a big thing. It brings remarkable feelings of freedom and ease to such an extent that some have thought of this as "enlightenment," although from our perspective there's still much more to evolve into.

Sheri: I was never very interested in consciousness because I thought that was an out of body thing. But then one day while doing yoga, my body woke up. That's the only way I can describe it. My body realized that it's made of infinite space. I was afraid this would make me less grounded, but it did exactly the opposite – I realized that emptiness was the true ground because it never changes. Since then, I've felt grounded in my body more than ever before.

- Meditate on the feeling of spaciousness in the body.
- Notice that spaciousness is the part of you that registers your own embodied experience. In other words, the spacious emptiness is You.
- Notice that you witness your body with eyes open during the day.

Stage 8: Oscillating

Stage Overview: Leaning into the discomfort of apparent opposites

- Subjective: Trying to hold self as finite and infinite
- Observable: Talks of experiencing and losing unity
- Relational: Relating alternately from personal or transpersonal self
- Systemic: Balancing personal needs and universal awareness in systems

Needs: To grow beyond fixating on polarities

Identity: I'm sometimes infinite, sometimes finite

"Life is strong and fragile. It's a paradox... It's both things, like quantum physics: It's a particle and a wave at the same time. It all exists all together." – Joan Jett

In Stage 7, the search for the ultimate sense of self results in the realization of consciousness as the infinitely spacious aspect of one's own being. Most assume that this will bring them happiness everlasting, but as usual, there's more to realize. For many, the feeling of being fractured is all the more obvious after the realization of infinite consciousness. Big existential questions arise, such as "I've realized the infinite side of myself, but what about my body? My mind? My emotions? My unique personality? How do these apparently different parts of myself go together?"

In Stage 8, there is a powerful drive to discover the unity between the apparently separate parts of ourselves. Some feel this as a yearning to come home to oneself; others as a yearning for unity with being or the universe. Some yearn for unity between "higher self" and "lower self," others for unity between self and a supreme or divine other. In any case, to cultivate this new awareness, most people find themselves naturally oscillating in identifying with different Domains until all are woven so closely in awareness that they are experienced together without conflict.

Stage 8 is about holding the tension of sometimes feeling infinite, expanded, or free, and sometimes feeling extremely limited, contracted, or confined. It can feel like alternating between "got it" and "lost it." This often happens when people go to a meditation retreat and feel expanded, then come home and encounter the limits of ordinary life. The pressures of daily life often contribute to feeling our realization of consciousness is sometimes overshadowed.

Some experience Stage 8 a little differently. Instead of oscillating between "got it" and "lost it", the experience is more like a gradual awakening of consciousness simultaneous with awareness of being human. In both cases, the challenge is to allow and feel the "bothness" of infinite and finite.

Once we clearly experience being both limitless and limited and are able to feel these poles together at the same time, we come to know ourselves as a paradox, and we feel a sense of impossibility that we are both. This feeling can be described as existential angst, yearning, or core wound. If we misinterpret this feeling as something wrong, we can easily resist it, which delays unity realization. However, once we choose to live and embrace this feeling, it becomes a secret doorway into a new life of fundamental wellness. In that new life, we are no longer fundamentally avoiding discomforts or paradox.

Stage 8 brings the capacity for "both/and" processing. Instead of fixating on one or another side of any duality, we learn to allow both. We start to see that we don't have to choose sides or add undue resistance to our life experiences. We can allow life to have its ups and downs, and we can allow all of that simultaneously. An example is when you see something one way, and another person sees the same thing in a completely different way. You're right *and* they're right. Both are right, even though they appear to be in conflict. Are you in conflict with apparent conflict? Or can you accept that life arises in apparent dualities?

As we relax, lean into, and actually embrace the tension of bothness in each moment, something magical happens. We discover that infinite and finite are one; that we ourselves and all our parts are one. Toward the end of Stage 8, you become adept at allowing and embracing dualities in yourself, others, and life. You see the both/and in all situations. You see that all exist together, and you become ready to experience unity in Stage 9.

Harris: I always felt the urge to be free, yet it seemed that being human always meant being bound up in limits. I would go on adventures, trying to feel free and unlimited, but there was always a limit, always something that made me feel trapped and small. Then a mentor helped me realize that both are true. That one insight completely changed me; I realized that I could choose to be both free AND bound, and I could stop fighting against limits.

> • Go into your day looking for how you relate to dualities. Good vs. bad: do you strongly identify with one or the other? Can you be both? Right vs. wrong: See if you can notice that things and people are both right AND wrong, depending on your perspective. Positive vs. negative: Notice that both are true at all times. Self vs. others: Can you get what you need AND support others to do the same? Free will vs. determinism: Notice that both are true.

Stage 8 - Consciousness

Location Description: Trying to hold the tension of being both finite and infinite

Needs: To embrace the discomfort of being your human self and limitless existence

"Before we can hold the immense range from infinite to finite, we tend to move back and forth between these two extremes."
— Margit Bantowsky

Especially after awakening as the boundless dimension of existence in Stage 7, the experience of being alternately limitless and confined in human limits can be confusing and uncomfortable. In our experience, such oscillations in identity are a necessary process of weaving together our personal identity with our transpersonal identity.

As we integrate our awareness of infinite consciousness and limited humanness, we encounter the strange feeling of bothness. Some feel bothness as a crucifixion, others as an impossible paradox. Even while the mind struggles with this, we can learn to relax in the midst of it all and embrace the totality. Toward the end of Stage 8, we become ok with this existential discomfort because we accept the fact that life is a package deal, both good and bad, infinite and finite. Here, we are no longer interested in maintaining our resistance to this perplexing fact or feeling. We can no longer will ourselves to do things in an attempt to change the fact that life always brings apparent duality. Remarkably, this sets us up for realizing unity.

Dale: I kept realizing consciousness and then apparently losing it. I had the distinct experience that I couldn't possibly be both infinitely free and extremely limited at the same time. How could both be true? I tried to figure this out, but my mind had no way to grasp the paradox. It was like a Zen koan that couldn't be solved. Then I got it: it can't be solved! There's no need to solve it. I'm just both and it doesn't matter that it makes no sense to my mind.

- Sit with eyes closed and rest as your awareness. Bring your attention to the feeling of being your body. Notice your awareness just being with your body. Notice any discomfort in holding the bothness of consciousness and body. Stay with this bothness a little longer each time.
- Sit silently with another person, gazing into each other's eyes. Allow and embrace whatever feelings are present. Notice yourself, notice the other, and notice what happens when you release the self/other duality.

Stage 8 - Uniqueness

Location Description: Identity alternates between personality and universal being

Needs: To embrace the paradox of bothness

"Always remember that you are absolutely unique. Just like everyone else." –Margaret Mead

Stage 8 highlights a sense of tension between our personality and our transpersonal nature. On one hand, each of us has our own very unique and specific ways of being and expressing ourselves, all of which makes us different from other humans. On the other hand, we've realized that we all share qualities of the infinite mystery in common. Sometimes we lean more toward our personal humanness, sometimes more toward our shared boundlessness. The key is learning to hold the tension of both. The practice of being with bothness is not to make existential tension go away because that amounts to resistance, which takes us further into fighting what is. We practice bothness to embrace the truth of life and to become at peace with both joy and sorrow, pain and pleasure, infinite and finite.

Eventually, we come to deeply accept and embrace life's extremes. We see that both sides of our nature are true, and we can be simultaneously both. It's this willingness to hold the "both/and" that propels us into the Unified Phase.

Ellen: For a long time, I thought that indulging my personality was taking me away from experiencing what's universal. But then I wasn't even really being my human self! Paradoxically, when I let myself be my personality more, I had more experiences of universal consciousness.

- Ask at least 3 of your friends and/or family members to tell you what your 3 top limits or challenges are. As they tell you what they see, practice not deflecting. Practice being completely receptive until they are done and then thank them. Just notice and feel your own reactions or responses. Be curious about where your reactions are coming from. If you are rejecting your own limits in any way, it's important to discover how to embrace them because they are part of who you are. Embracing our limits turns out to be very liberating. It's good to push our limits to a point, but once we know them, we can learn to understand them to best empower our gifts. Constantly trying to fix or transcend your limits may sound like a great ideal, but sooner or later you may discover that learning to cooperate with them makes you more effective.
- Ask the same people to tell you what they see as your top 3 gifts. Again, no deflecting, just accept the feedback and thank them. Otherwise, you are stopping yourself from owning the truth of who you are, which is the opposite of self-realization and self-actualization.
- Journal about other limits and challenges not mentioned by your friends. Write about how nothing is wrong about any of them and why each is perfect.

Stage 8 - Mind

Location Description: Trying to hold the paradox of known and unknown

Needs: To relax into the discomfort of endless mystery while yearning for understanding

"Across planes of consciousness, we have to live with the paradox that opposite things can be simultaneously true."
– Ram Dass

At stage 8, we begin finding the willingness, capacity, and desire to be with the tension of thinking mind and spacious knowingness. This often appears as a sort of competition for our attention; on one hand, we get absorbed in our thoughts; on the other hand, we are absorbed in the recognition of consciousness. To get to the point of knowing both simultaneously, we tend to oscillate between mind and consciousness until we eventually get that both are always part of our true nature. As our perceived divisions dissolve in Stage 9, we start to experience thoughts as waves within spacious knowingness.

Gary: I tended to move from one extreme to the other. I'd go on retreat, meditate a lot, and feel really expanded. Then I'd come home, get back to work, and feel like I totally lost it, especially when I got immersed in my mind. It really felt like I could have thoughts or emptiness, but not both. But I practiced holding them both together and found that I could have both at the same time. That started to resolve what seemed like a tug-of-war I'd been living in for years.

- Sit with eyes closed and rest as consciousness. After some time, bring your attention to your thoughts. Notice the bothness of consciousness and thoughts. Stay with this bothness a little longer each time until it's clear that consciousness is always present when thoughts are present.
- Practice being aware of your mind's tendency to try to figure everything out. Practice sitting in the feeling that life is mystery. Notice that both can be happening at the same time.
- Allow the tension of the difference between your thoughts and beliefs, and those of others. Become at home with those differences.

Stage 8 - Emotions

Location Description: Trying to hold the tension of unconditional love and personal emotions

Needs: To embrace the discomfort of being your human self and limitless existence

"Be universal in your love. You will see the universe to be the picture of your own being." – Sri Chinmoy

Once we've had an awakening to universal love, we experience the dance between personal emotions and universal love. Sometimes you feel love for everyone and everything. Sometimes you hate people. Sometimes you love someone but you're not sure if its them you love or their universal essence.

These oscillations continue until we are able to feel both at the same time without resisting or grasping for one side or the other. You might find yourself wondering how it's possible to love everything and everyone while simultaneously disliking someone. How can I feel love and hate at the same time? Is it ok to have these emotional polarities? Coming into Stage 8, we still struggle with such polarities. There's a feeling of pinch, impossibility, or paradox about the coexistence of apparent opposites. But as you move towards the end of Stage 8, you notice that even though polarities are challenging to feel, you actually want to feel them, so you can stop fighting with reality and experience union.

At Stage 8, radical embrace of the simultaneity of personal and universal as well as conflicting emotions is what helps push you over the line into the Unified Phase of your life. We emerge from Stage 8 knowing that all opposites can be here at the same time, whether or not it makes sense. We can allow ourselves to feel universal love and personal emotions, and we can choose to avoid relationships we don't find nourishing while still feeling love for those we don't like.

Herb: When I was growing up, it seemed like my parents either loved me or hated me. I never knew which way it was going to be. When I got older, I noticed that I either loved myself, or I was beating myself up for something. And I had the same disposition with others. Recently I've been able to hold a much broader range of emotions, and I can hold apparent opposites better. I can let myself be flawed and still love myself.

- Notice that your experience or intuition of universal love is present while your emotions go up and down. Notice that personal and universal simultaneously coexist.
- Practice radical self-embrace. Love yourself no matter how bad or unacceptable you think you are. Practice embracing all your aspects, both light and dark, both good and bad, pain and pleasure, infinite and finite, divine and human, by giving yourself permission to be all of who and what you are in each moment.

- Your presence itself brings love. Bring presence to your own emotions, and to the emotions of others. Bring presence to the feeling of paradox or conflict. Whatever your internal reactions may be, stay with what you feel. Later, you can find new ways to express what you feel, but for now, learn to be present with your emotional truth without trying to change it.

Stage 8 - Body

Location Description: Trying to hold awareness of body and spaciousness simultaneously

Needs: To relax into acceptance of being both physical and non-physical

"At the ultimate heart of the body, at the heart of the world, there is no solidity." – George Leonard

In Stage 8, we experience a tension between finite body and infinite emptiness. How can we be both material and non-material at the same time? While this appearance is highly perplexing to our mind, it doesn't change the fact that both appear to be true. As part of our process to resolve the apparent paradox, our sense of identity flips between being the body and being the emptiness of our transpersonal nature. Through these oscillations we develop the capacity to hold the tension of both of these aspects of our nature simultaneously.

It's important to note that holding the tension of being both infinite and finite requires the willingness to be deeply present with existential discomfort. For many, at the bottom of everything, it feels like something is a little off, or wrong, or paradoxical in a way that doesn't go together. Questions arise like "How can I be both my body and my consciousness at the same time? My body is so limited and small and my consciousness is so huge. How can I be both?" We go through oscillations between the personal and universal aspects of our being as we sort out how to integrate these seemingly incompatible layers of ourselves. With practice and skilled assistance, we learn to simply hang out with that feeling of paradox and let it be present.

Nancy: One day I was meditating and I felt my body floating in vast spaciousness. It was totally strange, almost like I was in outer space, yet fully here on Earth at the same time. That started happening more often, and after many months of that, I notice it's always true, even when I'm not in meditation.

- Feel your body and consciousness together simultaneously. Ask yourself: If I had to feel this bothness for the rest of eternity, would that be ok? If not, why not?
- Journal: What are your objections to being both a physical person and limitless being?

Section 4: Developing in the Unified Phase

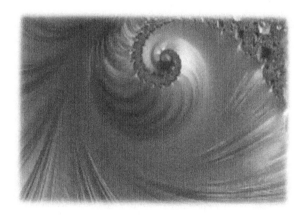

"Quantum physics reveals a basic oneness of the universe."
– Erwin Schrodinger

The Unified Phase spans the range from Stage 9 through Stage 12. It starts with a life-changing shift that occurs when the fractured perspectives and existential yearning felt toward the end of the Dual Phase yields to a new sense of wholeness, oneness, and fundamental wellness.

In the Unified Phase, all Domains are known as whole, unified, connected, and integrated. In this Phase we have dropped out of fundamental resistance to what is, and awakened into union with life and self. This transition is experienced as far more profound than the shift of identity into consciousness in Stage 7. This is a shift into seeing infinite and finite as a single thing. It becomes a new platform for life that is radically different from that in the Dual Phase.

Part of what happens during the Unified Phase is that we notice there's no boundary between "inside" and "outside". The experience of unity makes it clear that absolute and relative, personal and impersonal, inside and outside, are all the same. This is a truly massive shift in perspective that will radically change your life for the better because it will make you feel deeply part of the world.

There is usually a honeymoon period in Stage 9 while the realization is dawning, being recognized, and owned. This is followed by a whole-being transformation in Stage 10 that, through a series of core healings, integrates the unity realization with the past wounds and conditionings in the Dual Phase. Later in the Unified phase we find ourselves liberated into life, living our full potential in service to the world. At the end of the Unified Phase, we are challenged to surrender all sense – even all awakened sense – of separate self.

Stage 9: Embodied Unity

Stage Overview: Non-separate realization brings immediate wholeness, wellness, and presence

- Subjective: Experiencing wholeness as everything, nothing, and personal self
- Observable: Operating with persistent awakened presence
- Relational: Realizing the unity of self and other
- Systemic: Synergizing with systems

Needs: To own and claim unity realization for oneself and have that realization recognized and confirmed by others

Identity: I am Everything, Nothing, and me

"The point is to unify the opposites, both positive and negative, by discovering a ground which transcends and encompasses them both. And the ground is unity consciousness." – Ken Wilber

Prior to Stage 9, most people's lives revolve around the underlying sense that something is fundamentally wrong or missing. For some, it feels we're always experiencing parts of ourselves, never all of ourselves. On some level, the Dual Phase is like living in a perpetual struggle with self, others, and/or life – a struggle to resist, change, or fix what is, or to win a battle between one side of a polarity over another. This struggle causes a constant underlying distress, anxiety, confusion, or separateness. If the need to realize unity continues unfulfilled for years, it can turn into existential emptiness or despair.

From our perspective, there is nothing wrong with the struggles that lead us to unity. The Dual Phase can be extremely challenging, but necessary. As we live through it, we learn about many parts of ourselves and the larger realities we live in. All of these experiences are natural aspects of our evolution because they propel us forward while forming the basis for realizing unity. Without knowing duality, we cannot know unity.

The oscillations between personal and transpersonal that happen in Stage 8 cause a deep yearning for wholeness and oneness. This prompts us to accept the paradoxical tension of infinite and finite at the core of our being. Early in Stage 9, we learn to fully embrace the feeling of personal and transpersonal together as the current feeling of our whole-being self. This gives us a platform from which we can embrace all opposites, including perfect and imperfect, good and bad, right and wrong, light and dark. This is the secret trap door to awakening into the Unified Phase at Stage 9: when you are ready to relax around resistance, face, deeply feel, and embrace all opposites – including your own human and your own infinite being at the same time – you are ready for the profound union with yourself that simultaneously reveals your unity with everything.

We come to Stage 9 when we realize that everything we have loved and hated, everything we have strived for or resisted, is all part of our very self. Seeing this, our war with life drops away, and we awaken into an unprecedented intimacy with all things. Suddenly (or, for some, gradually), we realize with wonder that everything is one, and oneness is who and what we are. As this unity dawns, we notice that there is no experience in any Domain that can overshadow our knowingness that All is One.

"When we try to pick out anything by itself, we find it hitched to everything else in the universe."– John Muir

Some describe this realization as "I am everything and everything is me." Others feel it as "everything is everything". The essence of this realization is that, despite the appearance of everyone and everything being separate, it's also true that everyone and everything are also one unified reality. This may seem an impossible paradox, yet the realization makes this fact clear, despite the mind's struggle to understand how such a thing could be possible.

The realization of unity changes the very structure of your awareness for the rest of your life. The structure changes from fundamental duality and polarity to fundamental unity and oneness. The discovery of unity releases you from seeking to find it, which in turn catapults you into the present. You are no longer searching for yourself because you found yourself. You realize that you are everything (the universe), nothing (spacious being), and you (your personal self) all as one.

Those who cross into unity experience a fundamental

wellness of being that is hard to describe. We can't understand it based on our previous experience, because all previous experience happened on the basis of a sense of wrongness, separateness, or incompleteness. When unity dawns, it becomes a new platform of wholeness and wellness for all experience. We spontaneously see how all things gross and subtle fit together. We know that all is right and perfect, even while it can look and feel very imperfect. The relief of this realization is profound, because we are no longer busy resisting, ignoring, or fixing our reality. We are no longer pushing away what we don't want and grasping for what we do want. We are simply and obviously living in a depth of boundless being that is effortlessly unified with our humanness.

The need at Stage 9 is to recognize this unity, acknowledge that it has dawned, and own the truth of it. But at this point it really helps to have confirmation, because it's difficult to know without outside reflection if what shifted was specifically what we call Embodied Unity. With recognition and confirmation from another who has been through this awakening, the realization itself can land more deeply until it becomes an unshakeable knowingness. It brings with it an unexpected confidence in being; a certainty that we belong because we are life itself.

This transition is just the beginning of a longer process of reconciling the recognition of unity with the past conditioning based in the perception of duality. Toward the end of Stage 9, the consequences of this shift begin to make clear that we must heal our whole-being belief in fundamental separateness based on our direct realization of non-separateness. Over time, we learn how to live and deeply embody the realized oneness.

The shift from Dual to Unified brings a previously unknown form of whole-being confidence and a steadiness in relation to life. We are no longer running from things because we have chosen to accept life on its own terms, with all its ups and downs. We have chosen to feel what we don't like because it's part of what is real and true. We have matured into the recognition that we are both limited and limitless, that we are both good and bad, that we have the power to create and destroy. We are no longer hypnotized into resisting apparent dualities because it's obvious that all opposites are connected. We have learned to stand in paradoxes that can feel like crucifixion, and through this, know unity.

The realization of unity not only brings a basic form of whole-being maturity, it also brings the capacity for whole-being patience. This is not patience born of tolerating what we don't like; it's patience born of fully and spontaneously embracing discomfort as a natural part of life. It gives us the capacity to stay deeply present with what is, whether we like it or not. And that gives us the ability to accomplish whatever we want to achieve in life. Seeing that we can hold the existential discomfort of infinite and finite, we get that we can hold any particular discomfort and be ok. There is no longer any reason to let discomfort stop us from fulfilling our purpose. We are no longer making decisions based on what we don't want to feel, such as failure or rejection. Discomfort is part of being alive, and we are no longer running from it.

The reason we call Stage 9 Embodied Unity is to distinguish

it from awakenings that are mostly in the dead or don't include the body or other personal Domains. If the unity one experiences does not include one's limited humanness, it is still in the Dual Phase. Those who fall into embodied unity realization have chosen to embrace their body, their humanness, and their limitlessness, and see the fruitlessness of any attempt to do otherwise.

David: One evening at a party, I realized that something was bothering me, but I didn't know what it was. As I sat with it, I realized that I felt like everyone else was on the playing field of life, but I was in the bleachers. I saw that what had kept me in that feeling my whole life was that I was rejecting my own pain. Suddenly, I wanted to feel everything, including my pain. I wanted to feel whatever was real for me, more than anything. I just wanted to be fully here. In the next moment, I felt like I fell off a cliff. I waited for days, expecting to hit some sort of bottom. But then I realized that falling into life was my new normal. I had realized the unity I'd been seeking for 25 years! From that point on, my whole life transformed completely.

- Explore the stability of your unity realization. Is it there all the time? Is it there when you're not checking to see if it's there? Is it present even when you wonder or doubt if it's there?
- Get help from an expert to own the shift you went through.
- Tell a friend about your experience of this shift. Notice any hesitation. Practice standing in your truth about where you find yourself.

Stage 9 - Consciousness

Location Description: Consciousness is experienced as unified with personal domains

Needs: To acknowledge and own the union of consciousness with my humanness

"Form is emptiness, emptiness is form." – Buddha

In Stage 9, Embodied Unity, there's a realization that infinite consciousness and finite humanness are non-separate. My personal Domains are non-separate from existence. Therefore, I am part of everything! This revelation is profound, to say the least. Once this realization is stable, there is no doubt about the fundamental union with life. The only doubt is how to live this realization and how to reconcile this new perspective with our conditioned assumptions of separateness since childhood, which most people around us operate from.

It can feel as though all the parts of us that were fighting are suddenly aligned as a single unified reality. This brings a feeling of immense simplicity and clarity. It's not necessarily clarity about a particular thing, but this clarity lends itself to everything from that point forward. There's a feeling of being expansive, whole, and inclusive of all things, and that nothing is separate. It becomes clear there's no need to fight with life or any part of ourselves because everything we previously resisted was just a part of self. And obviously, no one wins in a battle with oneself. We realize that we used to spend huge amounts of energy and attention fighting with ourselves. This recognition is the beginning of an enormous relaxation that we could not have previously known or imagined was possible.

This shift of whole-life perspective brings a sense of immediacy. For some, there is a sudden, almost deafening lack of resistance or conflict. The noise and activity of seeking to find a place where we can feel totally at home has stopped. Suddenly, we realize we *are* home.

Emma: First I realized that consciousness is in the body and the body is also in consciousness. Then I had trouble sorting out which was in which; they both just inhabited each other, they both existed together, there was no choosing one or the other. Then I realized they're the same thing! That brought an immense relaxation into unity. The feeling of whole-being relief was absolutely incredible. From that moment on, I knew the unity in everything and everyone and fundamental wellness became my new reality.

- Sit in meditation on the blissful unity of consciousness and your total humanness. Enjoy the fact that you no longer need to do anything to know this fundamental wellness of being.
- Outside meditation, notice that the sense of unity continues through all experience.

Stage 9 - Uniqueness

Location Description: Personality is realized as a non-separate expression of being

Needs: To acknowledge and own the union of my personality and being

"Everything is one and I am one with it."– Ruth Bernhard

The realization that our uniqueness is an integral expression of life is profound. We see that our uniqueness is actually needed as part of the mystery of life. A flower may have a strange shape, and we may think there's something wrong with it, but later we discover it's designed to attract a particular insect. Like that, each of our strange quirks has a purpose we discover later, as we embrace and explore what makes us different.

Understanding the value of our uniqueness encourages us to live our gifts and our limits without shame or defense. By releasing our attachments to self-negation, we discover the power to own our truth. This liberates us to be far more effective at bringing our gifts to the world.

Embracing our uniqueness also helps us to understand and cooperate with the uniqueness of others. Each of us plays our own role in the much larger system of humanity. The realization that we are not separate from anything makes it clear we are not separate from others, and that we must learn to honor others and cooperate in ways that bring fulfillment to our unique purpose.

Barb: For most of my life, I thought there was something wrong with me. Something about who I was seemed basically wrong. I felt like everyone else was happy together, but I was banished. But then I started to get that actually, that wrong feeling wasn't confirmation of how bad I was; it was just the feeling of rejecting myself! As soon as I saw that, I started loving myself. And then, one day, I dropped into myself in a way I could never have anticipated. I simply became who I am.

- When relating with others, speak your personal truth in the moment (with self-responsibility). Be aware of your fears of not fitting in, yet dare to have a different opinion and be your unique self anyway.
- Journal about your purpose in life. If you could accomplish just one thing before your life is over, what would that be?
- Journal about how you see working with others to accomplish your purpose.

Stage 9 - Mind

Location Description: Personal thoughts are known as aspects of being

Needs: To acknowledge and own the mind's unity with being

"To the mind that is still, the whole universe surrenders."
– Lao Tsu

In Stage 9, our thoughts can no longer dislodge us from the

knowingness that we are unified with life. Thoughts appear far less dense then previously because our sense of self is no longer primarily based in our mind; our sense of self is now both personal and universal as one. This allows us to think in much more fluid ways than we previously knew. We start to see the world in wholes, rather than just parts. Holistic thinking starts to dominate, deeply affecting all our ideas and beliefs. The shift into unity radically opens us to new views of self, others, and life.

By approaching thinking from a much larger perspective, we find ourselves less fixated on particular thoughts or thought patterns. We notice that thoughts are a way to process the infinite possibilities inherent in every situation. Stage 9 imparts the capacity for deep presence and patience in the midst of thinking. We don't have to react to every thought as if it's the only truth or viewpoint. This frees us to think in more practical and creative ways. It also frees us to see that our mind is here to serve us, not the other way around.

Bill: One weekend I decided to get out of my head and go hiking in the woods. I sat on a rock and just listened to the wind moving through the trees. After some time, I realized that the sound of the wind was like my thoughts and it was all just part of the mystery that animates me and everything. That realization turned out to be the biggest shift in my life, and it never left. I know I'm part of everything.

- Observe your thinking... write down the thought patterns that occur most frequently. A pattern could be "I try to be more positive," "I think about worst-case scenarios," or "I think about what's wrong with me", etc. When any thoughts that fit this pattern come into your awareness, notice it's just one of your standard patterns and notice that you are larger than that.
- When talking with others, notice your own reactions to their thoughts. See if you can discover what's under your reactions. Do these thoughts bring up uncomfortable feelings? Are you ok with that?

Stage 9 - Emotions

Location Description: Feeling emotions as waves of being

Needs: To acknowledge and own the unity of emotions with being

"People can be apart physically but they can still have an emotional connection." – Steve Coogan

The above quote beautifully illustrates the fact that our emotions are not separate from those of others. At Stage 9, we realize that personal and universal, self and other, are all a part of the same thing. We can no longer fixate on the fight against "bad" feelings by trying to transform them into "good" feelings. At this point, it's about *all* feelings. In our jigsaw puzzle analogy, the pieces have all come together, informing all our feelings with wholeness. There are still lines between the pieces in the jigsaw, representing the ways our previous duality-based conditioning can still make us feel separate even though we've already realized non-separateness. This is a paradox that gets worked out over the rest of the Unified Phase.

Here, we realize our emotions are non-separate waves in the ocean of being, our feelings are not separate from those of others, and our heart is not separate from life. We are all part of a vast, interconnected reality pervaded by the experience of fundamental intimacy with everything. At the same time, we still find ourselves resisting certain emotions out of the force of habit. The rub between our realization of unity and our emotional habits move us toward a deeper healing in Stage 10.

Karen: I always assumed that my emotions made me petty and that I'd be better off without them. People around me thought I was cold and aloof. But when my brother passed away unexpectedly, I cried for a long time. In my grief, I reconnected with my family and my own heart. At one point, I had a big shift and realized that feeling my deepest emotions had brought me home to myself. I felt like my brother saved my life when he died.

- What is your least favorite emotion? Practice feeling that emotion in yourself while embracing it with love.
- What emotion is most challenging for you to be with in others? Practice being present with others when they express that feeling. Watch your old patters that used to cause you to react in such situations. Practice developing patience and compassion with yourself and others around emotions.

Stage 9 - Body

Location Description: Realizing the unity of body and being

Needs: To acknowledge and own the body's unity with being

"In the stillness of your presence, you can feel your own formless and timeless reality as the unmanifest life that animates your physical form. You can then feel the same life deep within every other human and every other creature. You look beyond the veil of form and separation. This is the realization of oneness."
– Eckhart Tolle

In Stage 8 we felt and embraced the tension of being body and emptiness. In Stage 9 this tension comes to a deep resolution. We call Stage 9 "Embodied Unity" because this is where we begin recognizing our body as a non-separate manifestation of Being. The resolution of body and emptiness is not in our mind; it's in the noticing that there never was separation between these aspects of who we are in the first place. We notice that the appearance of fundamental separation was an illusion based in the limits of our perception. By simply being present with these two parts of ourselves without trying to change how that feels, unity dawns.

In the Dual Phase, there is a feeling of being fractured or split into parts in a way we can't fully understand. But as we pass into the Unified Phase, it's as if our whole life starts coming into focus. In the Body Domain, this shift is often felt as a kind of landing or crystallization into a new, unified sense of self. Suddenly there's a feeling of seamless wholeness; the body no longer feels separate from any of the other Domains, such as consciousness, but also the body begins to feel non-separate from others and the rest of the world. There's a clear sense that body and world are simply aspects of the same thing.

What propels people into the enormous shift of unity is the deep desire to be fully here as both infinite awareness and physical form together, no matter how that feels. That feeling is unique for everyone. However that feels to you, you'll find yourself at peace when you accept and embrace it. When embracing your whole being and living fully is what you truly want, you'll be ready for this shift.

Lilly: For me, this felt like a coming down and into my body like a spaceship landing. It felt like I was dropping down, starting in my head, down through my throat, into my heart, into my belly, down into my legs, and landing deep into the ground. It was consciousness coming down and into my body, one cell at a time. Simultaneously, I felt wholeness coming online. Instead of oscillating between exclusive identification with body, then exclusive identification with infinity, I felt my awareness came down and landed in my body, and I was one. After that shift, there was no longer a seeking, grasping, wanting the physical or wanting the emptiness. There was a joy to fully be embodied here in the present; there's presence here within the physical realm while also experiencing a sense of the vast infinite.

- Make your body the object of your loving attention for a while. When you don't like how your body feels, devote yourself to staying deeply present with the feelings, embracing each one as yourself.
- Notice your reactions to being physically present with others. Explore your reactions and see if you can discover what is beneath each one. What do you notice you don't want to feel when you're with others? How much does your own childhood conditioning play out in physical interactions?

Stage 10: Transforming

Stage Overview: Core duality-based conditioning surfaces for healing

- Subjective: Awakened unity allows healing deepest wounds and dualities
- Observable: Displays fallibility with kindness and humor; periodic meltdowns
- Relational: Intimacy prompts healing deepest relational wounding and conditioning
- Systemic: Brings core healing to systems

Needs: To thoroughly heal and realign with realized wholeness

Identity: I am everything healing my humanness

"Owning our story can be hard but not nearly as difficult as spending our lives running from it." –Brene Brown

The fundamental wellness realized at Stage 9 matures into a whole-being need to re-integrate all Domains and Views from the new unified, holistic perspective. Everything in our being that has not been examined on the new platform of wholeness must be unpacked and healed until the unity realized at Stage 9 can become fully embodied in Stage 10 and beyond. There's been plenty of healing prior to this point, but we call Stage 10 "Transforming" because at this point, the healing process goes all the way to the very core of our being. This was previously impossible while we were still rejecting ourselves, avoiding feelings we didn't like, and lacking the ground of unified awareness we needed to feel safe enough to permit such core healing.

Stage 10 usually starts with a lot of healing of past unresolved trauma and conditioning that arose from life in the Dual Phase. Because we are now ready, willing, strong enough, and not confined by a limited sense of self, life supplies the opportunities we need to bring the healing process to an integrated resolution. Our sense of self is now vast enough to hold everything. All previous tactics for avoiding core healing will be out the window here. Everything in your internal and external life that is not aligned with who you are is up for spontaneous realignment; every rejected part of you must come home and be fully unified. It takes time to transition your whole being from the old fractured worldview to the new unified one, so be brave and patient; know that it's totally worth going through this.

The good news is that you get credit for all the prior healing work you've done. To whatever degree you've come to know yourself and healed your past patterns and conditioning, you won't be blindsided by what you find still deeper that remains to be healed. In the past, it was too threatening to dissolve the old conditioned patterns because your sense of self was so identified with them. The difference now is that your entire being demands deep and lasting resolution.

And this time you have all the resources you need to maintain your sense of wholeness while you allow this deep transformation to work its way through all your Domains, all your relationships, and all the ways you bring yourself into to the world. This transformation process will scour and realign all of who you are including your roots through your family and your ancestry. It's not that you haven't gone through hundreds of other healing events before, but this time each event ends with a clear sense of resolution. After dozens of such events, you'll begin to experience the liberation we describe at Stage 11.

Please note that nobody heals 100% as they are moving beyond Stage 10, but we put the line at 80% healed because that's enough to allow the deep actualization of Stage 11. What remains after Stage 10 are like faint echoes of the old conditionings that may arise from time-to time, but no longer inhibit you from being who you are.

Chris: Shortly after my shift into unity, I started having these moments when issues I thought I was done with kept coming back. But this time, instead of trying to fix them, I just hung out with them. Each time I did that, I would see right back to the moment when the issue started, and I could feel my love and presence healing it. After that happened a bunch of times, I felt completely transformed... not into something else or something better, but into who I was designed to be.

- To help release old relationship issues, let go of defensive mechanisms and allow yourself to feel the other person's hurt. If you feel some responsibility, apologize. Even if you believe you had nothing to do with causing pain for another person, feel their pain and empathize. Love, presence, empathy, and compassion bring healing.
- Find ways to keep your whole system feeling nourished and supported. Take walks in nature, take baths, sit in meditation, whatever helps you feel good is a resource while your system is rapidly rewiring itself.

Stage 10 - Consciousness

Location Description: Awareness illuminates and transforms deep wounds and conditioning

Needs: To release the habit of controlling awareness to avoid unhealed issues

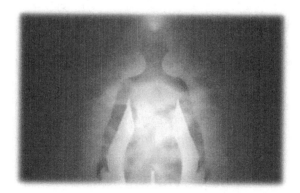

"The great solution to all human problems is individual inner transformation." – Vernon Howard

In Stage 10, consciousness is like a flashlight that descends into all our Domains, lighting up all dark, unconscious spaces to be embraced and welcomed into unity. All splits and outgrown conditionings must be revealed and healed. Despite the Stage 9 realization of seamless unity, the deepest splits that remain are our conditioned ways of holding our personal sense of self separate from others and the world. All conditioned habits of distracting our consciousness from whatever needs our attention will be dismantled here. By the time we are transitioning out of Stage 10, the old reasons we held ourselves separate are revealed and dissolved.

Stage 10 will also challenge any remaining tendency to hold our own consciousness separate from everything else. The apparent supremacy of the infinite will dissolve in the realization of non-separation with our human world of personal experience. Stage 9 showed us that consciousness IS the world and the world IS consciousness. Stage 10 prompts us to clear our past so we can act on that basis.

Katie: For a while, it felt like my consciousness was showing me every issue from my past in a relentless way. I'd deal with one thing, and up came the next thing. I was also put through major changes in my life circumstances that seemed related. I started to see how the outside of my life was changing because everything inside was changing. After months of that, it felt like I was living a whole new life. In my new life, I feel total alignment between inside and out because those feel like the same thing.

- As you go about your day, release any remaining control over where your attention wants to go. You may notice that you've been avoiding certain issues or discomforts. Practice not avoiding those things. Let your consciousness go where it naturally wants to go and see what it uncovers.
- When you find yourself in the midst of a challenging confrontation with your old patterns, use your stable realization of non-dual consciousness as an anchor. You might want to sit in meditation or simply turn attention to the obviousness of being.

Stage 10 - Uniqueness

Location Description: Fundamental healing of self-negation

Needs: To update how we express our personality from duality to unity

"Awakening is not changing who you are but discarding who you are not." – Deepak Chopra

Our habits of negating our unique personality and gifts are often so deeply rooted that most of the time we can't see the dynamics that hold these patterns in place. However, at Stage 10 we can no longer hide such dynamics from ourselves. All conditioned patterns are revealed, and all self-negation comes up for healing. Every form of fear-based self-enslavement is unearthed. Everything about your life that is no longer aligned with who you uniquely are will arise to be integrated. Finding self-alignment becomes paramount.

Our habits of negating ourselves or making ourselves more or less than others will also come for up healing. This includes all the ways we look down on others because they are different from us (including other species). In Stage 10, all of that starts being healed to the point where we can embrace it, love everyone's uniqueness, and experience others as part of the perfection of life.

By this stage, we become free enough of our conditioning to discover our unique inner guidance system. Everyone has their own way of sensing how it works for them to respond to life, and if one's unique inner guidance is not already clear, it becomes deeply important at Stage 10 to discover that and learn to live in deep self-alignment.

Anton: I spent most of my life not knowing what to do or what to trust in myself. I tried trusting other's opinions about what I should do, but that didn't work. I felt like a ship without a compass. But after I shifted into unity, I started to feel my body talking to me. I noticed that my body was trying to show me how to act. It was a challenge to let my body take the lead, but ever since then, I don't get stuck in my head about decisions. I just follow my body. I know that doesn't work for everyone, but it really works for me.

- Journal about the ways you have negated yourself your whole life. Take note of how you've done this in all Domains, even if only in subtle ways. When those old habits arise, love them, and make a new choice to love yourself.
- What relationships in your life need healing? Think about family, friends, and colleagues with whom you may have left things badly. These people are not separate from you; their pain in relation to you is part of your pain in relation to them. Find ways to bring healing to these relationships, starting with listening to their side and fully feeling their reality without deflecting or defending. Your presence and willingness to empathize will bring forms of healing and wellness that can't happen if you try to do all your healing work alone, subjectively.

Stage 10 - Mind

Location Description: Releasing self-deceiving beliefs

Needs: To update the mind's ways of functioning from duality to unity

"Be brave and take accountability for yourthoughts and beliefs."
– Jennifer Hyman

At Stage 10, all beliefs about self and life are challenged. You may find yourself asking 'Do I still believe this thought?' 'Is this belief aligned with who I am now?' All thoughts based on our previous assumption of fundamental separateness must be re-examined here. Life tends to supply us with other people who will question or challenge our thoughts and beliefs. At this Stage, we take those questions seriously and we have the strength to make whatever changes are necessary to come into deeply alignment with our own unique ways of thinking and believing.

Jim: I used to believe a lot of things that I never really thought very deeply about. Recently, I found myself wanting to get to the core of every one of them. Almost every day, I'd see another belief that I no longer actually believe. It felt like I was clipping the hedges of my mind. After some time, that process faded out, and my mind has felt so much less cluttered that I spend lots of time with my mind being very quiet. It's become obvious that having a quiet mind makes it a lot easier to think clearly!

- Question your core beliefs and assumptions; how many of them were formed when you were young? Do they all align with your current experience and understanding?
- Observe your thoughts about yourself and others. Do you subconsciously put yourself down? Do you subconsciously put others down? What do you get from those old patterns of thinking?

Stage 10 - Emotions

Location Description: Unified awareness enables core healing of emotional wounds and conditioning

Needs: To update our emotional ways of functioning from duality to unity

"It is beautiful to love and to be free at the same time."
— Anais Nin

Any emotions that have not yet been seen, accepted, and fully embraced will come up at this Stage to be welcomed home as part of our wholeness. Any old emotional wounds, issues, patterns, or constrictions that are still stuck in our system will demand to be seen and reintegrated. The potent force of wholeness from our unity realization can inspire these old issues to come up with some surprising energy at this point. Anything we're still avoiding might become a crisis in order to get our attention.

As we move through the healing of Stage 10, we become more relaxed and at home in ourselves. We are no longer pushing away discomforts. This feels much more easeful, and gives us more patience with life's challenges, providing a new platform of presence in our relationships. We discover a new ability to allow our emotions to flow. We also learn to balance our own boundaries and needs while being supportive of others.

A crucial key in the ability to deeply heal and move into Stage 11 is our willingness to be truly vulnerable, at least in relationships we trust. We must be willing to hear and feel how others experience us, and receive reflections about our gifts and limits, warts and all. Until we can truly be who we are, both good and bad, and without defense, we are still holding a subtle separation from other humans that can only be healed in relationship. By stage 10, we are secure enough in our own being that we can allow uncomfortable feelings to arise and we can allow past identities to dissolve. If there are no relationships we can trust, we will be driven to find them. Until we do, we won't be able to fully heal ourselves or our relationship with life because others are part of who we are and we need them to fully see ourselves.

Carlos: I've always been emotionally defended; I think I got that from my father. I thought that was the right way to be. But after two divorces and a major awakening experience, that old pattern started to break down. I could no longer pretend my feelings didn't matter. I found myself becoming unreasonably sad or inexplicably happy, and it was actually ok. I still have some of the old tendencies, but I feel a lot more emotionally free.

- Journal about what stops you from expressing the depth of your emotions. How did that pattern start? How has withholding your feelings served you in the past, and what ways is it no longer helping you?
- Share your explorations around this with a close ally and ask for their help to express your true feelings when they sense you're holding back. This can't be done safely in all relationships, so do this with those you feel safe with.
- What emotions are hard for you to experience in yourself? What emotions are hard for you to witness in others? Practice feeling those difficult emotions. This will help you end the habit of running from what you feel.
- Is shame an issue for you? See if you can get to the bottom of it by exploring why you believe there's something wrong with you. If you look for it, you'll see that you've always been a doing your best, and that you're only human, just like everyone else.

Stage 10 - Body

Location Description: Healing and transforming deep physical conditioning

Needs: To discover what duality-based patterns prevent the embodiment of unity

"Wellness is the complete integration of body, mind, and spirit – the realization that everything we do, think, feel, and believe has an effect on our state of well-being." – Greg Anderson

Many people coming into Stage 10 have done a lot of work to release stuck patterns and energies in the body. But prior to realizing unity, there's a limit to how much of our previous issues and conditioning we can fully resolve, because we felt too unsafe to notice and feel everything required for deep healing to happen. Once we pass through the realization of wholeness at Stage 9, we feel safe and vast enough to remain present with whatever arises. At Stage 10, whatever wasn't dealt with prior to this point will come up to be fully met and released.

In the Dual Phase, we were unable to hold infinite and finite together consistently. In the Unified Phase, we're able to experience infinite boundlessness while going through deep healing. This provides far more space for these things to come up to be seen and welcomed and loved back into this whole. It's our grounded, spacious wholeness that gives us sufficient safety and space to allow this integrative transformation to happen in the body as well as the other Domains.

As the healing proceeds, the awakened emptiness begins to permeate our entire body, becoming a transparency or porousness that shines through the stickiness of personal limits. As the transparency increases, it permits even more of the old conditioning to be dissolved. Later in Stage 10, we start to notice the body's inherent wisdom about our actions and behaviors. We see and accept that we are amazingly powerful and intelligent beings.

Amy: My experience was of consciousness coming down in the body again... but this time, it felt like a flashlight coming down through my head; this bright light trying to inhabit my body and every nook and cranny. Every shadow that was yet to be seen was being illuminated so it could be integrated as part of the whole. Down into my arms, my heart, anything that was left untouched, unwelcomed, or unhealed was up to be seen. After months of that, I started to feel outrageously free.

- Ask your body what it needs to become free of the past. Then do what you can to fulfill those needs.
- Practice moving from your body; let your body respond to life as it wants to. Dare to release your mind from the position of ultimate decider.
- Find activities that help create space in the body: yoga, breathing techniques, dance, or other forms of exercise like running, swimming, or lifting weights. Bring breath to areas of the body to help release tension or dense areas.

Stage 11: Individuating

Stage Overview: Fundamentally untangled and liberated into life

- Subjective: Clarifying deepest purpose through living unity
- Observable: Consistently makes choices in alignment with purpose
- Relational: Embodying one's uniqueness in relating
- Systemic: Enhancing systems with unique gifts

Needs: To adjust to post-transformation life and live your unique purpose or function

Identity: I am Everything expressing through my human uniqueness

"The hero in each of us is required to answer the call of individuation." – James Hollis

While many feel the impulse to start individuating at Stage 4, we call Stage 11 "Individuating" because at this point, the emphasis is on fully embodying the truth of your uniqueness. And we can't fully embody our gifts while we're still mired in the issues of our past and experiencing ourselves as a separate, limited person. But as we emerge from the detangling process of Stage 10, we start to experience a remarkable freedom from the binding influence of our early conditioning and limited sense of self. We start individuating beyond the limits of the family and culture we grew up in.

The more deeply you live your truth, the more you automatically create a template for others to do the same for themselves and with each other. In Stage 11, you are increasingly driven by your own being to live your own path, no matter how threatening, different, or scary that may appear to you or to those around you. In Stage 11, your gifts are compelled to come forth and be lived in the world. You are being strongly impelled to prioritize and do what you're here to do. We highly recommend that you follow.

At this point, you're healed enough to begin living beyond yourself. You can see others without having your own stuff get in the way, and you can see yourself from others' perspectives without becoming defensive. Here, your entire sense of self is becoming less important than your need to serve others. It's this need to give service that compels us to discover how to move from independence to interdependence. We see we are part of a larger system of humanity and feel compelled to find our rightful place in it.

We need to mention that words like "serving" and "purpose" can be triggering for some, because it may sound like a pressure to be some sort of saint or super person. To us, living our truth can be as simple as cooking, painting, or just being loving. Whatever is in our personal nature to be or do, we'll be impelled to be or do without self-conflict at this stage.

Jon: I felt like I'd been hacking my way through a jungle all my life, and that activity had become a huge part of my life and identity. But after a series of incredibly challenging healings and transformations, that whole feeling stopped. I felt like I walked out of the jungle and into an endless clearing. It was astonishing. I had no idea this level of freedom was possible.

- Journal: What is my deepest longing? What do I most value? What really matters to me? What am I really here to give?
- Contemplate: What holds me back from living my full purpose with passion?

Stage 11 - Consciousness

Location Description: Deeply embodied presence in most situations

Needs: To turn outward and serve the world with unified consciousness

"The gift of presence is a rare and beautiful gift. To come - unguarded, undistracted - and be fully present, fully engaged with whoever we are with at that moment."
– John Eldredge

As we emerge from the transformation in Stage 10, most of our wounds and triggers have resolved. We feel untangled from that web and discover we now have the capacity to be who we are without fundamental internal conflicts and constraints. In Stage 11 we are free to be deeply embodied and present in most situations without running from anything we feel or experience.

In Stage 11, we become so liberated to be who we are that it frees our consciousness to go wherever it needs to go. We can bring our presence into any situation, staying with whatever arises. The more we release our resistance to life, the more we are present to what is.

Jill: I feel like my awareness is no longer sticky. It stays with things just as long as is needed, and then it moves on without needless attachments. To say the least, that's a completely new way of operating for me and it's a lot nicer.

- Journal: What experiences are still hard for me to stay present with?
- During your day, practice staying present with experiences you find difficult.

Stage 11 - Uniqueness

Location Description: Liberated to live unique truth

Needs: To discover how to express your personality without self-negation

"You change the world by being yourself." – Yoko Ono

Once our wounds have been fundamentally healed and integrated, we find ourselves liberated to be our unique self in the world. The release from conditioned encumbrances frees us to focus on what we're really here for. Despite our fears, we take our unique gifts into the world. Because we are no longer stopping or negating ourselves, we are liberated to manifest what we're here to be, express, and create. When expressing or creating from this kind of liberated space, what we bring forth starts to become free from the need to resolve shadow issues from the past or make it about ourselves.

Most of us are not familiar with living so freely because we're so used to operating from our conditioned beliefs. But Stage 11 brings challenges that force us to come out despite our fears and be who we are. Some may hate us for living our truth, others will love us. But living in integrity with yourself turns out to be far more effective, profitable, and easy than using your energy to stop your truth and your passion. At this stage there's an unwillingness to compromise your uniqueness no matter what the fears.

Stage 11 has a uniqueness theme because if we're not already clear about our unique gifts and purpose, life will challenge us to get clear. Some will realize that their purpose is to manifest specific things; others are here to offer unique functions; yet others are here to emanate qualities of being. Whatever your purpose, if it's not already clear, you'll be prompted to find it, clarify it, and live it. Please note that purpose can – and usually does – change. And that we all have many purposes and functions. So this is not about living up to some ideal, it's just about fully being who we are.

Robert: For a long time, I thought the point of awakening my consciousness was to have some sort of illumined or uplifted experience. But for me, awakened consciousness eventually brought me into who I'm here to be. I've always been an engineer, but now I get that my deeper purpose is to engineer positive social change using technology. It's hard transitioning from my job writing code to my true purpose, but I feel like I can't waste any more time not doing what I'm here to do.

- Journal: What am I afraid might happen if I fully express my unique purpose and gifts?
- Every day, remind yourself why you are here, and spend as much time as you can working to fulfill your own unique calling, even if it's only ten minutes.

Stage 11 - Mind

Location Description: Liberated from internal chatter to think clearly and authentically

Needs: To discover how to think authentically

"Live your beliefs and you can turn the world around."
– Henry David Thoreau

After we have gone through the de-conditioning of Stage 10, we are released from the old cobwebs of conditioned mental patterns and our thinking becomes more individuated. We feel empowered to express our unique thoughts and bring them to life in our work. We also find we're no longer tripped up by others' thought patterns and beliefs. We can see right through those patterns, appreciate the perfection of them, and dare to express our different views without getting stuck or re-identified with them. The more we do this, the more we notice the powerful, liberating effect this has, especially on those who have been imprisoned their whole lives by their own and others' beliefs.

Stage 11 also brings a new level of curiosity and flexibility to our thinking. We can also process more subtle and complex ideas. We are able to transcend old ways of thinking and be completely open to how our mind wants to work in the moment. We can have a thought and be fully prepared to throw it out, but equally prepared to see what it wants to show us.

Erin: I thought my crazy ways of thinking were just not that important. But I'm starting to get that I have a very unique vision of how everything that appears lifeless is just a small part of something bigger that's alive. I'm afraid to write about it, but I think it's part of why I'm here.

- Journal: What is unique about my particular worldview? What's unique about my thoughts and beliefs? Are there particular thoughts or beliefs I still avoid or identify with?
- When your views are different from those of others, speak out when that feels authentic. It doesn't matter if you're "right" or have the "best" ideas; it only matters that you express your authentic opinions.

Stage 11 - Emotions

Location Description: Continuous unconditional self-love

Needs: To discover how to live and express unconditional love in a world of limits and conditions

"Unconditional love really exists in each of us. It is part of our deep inner being. It is not so much an active emotion as a state of being. It's not 'I love you' for this or that reason, not 'I love you if you love me.' It's love for no reason, lovewithout an object." – Ram Dass

In Stage 11, we experience the wellness of deep unconditional self-love. And self-love automatically translates into deep unconditional love of others. It doesn't mean we love everybody the same way, it just means that on the universal level, we experience love for all people. On the personal level we experience various degrees of love and annoyance with different people. At this stage, we experience no conflict between these two levels.

It's also important to mention that no matter how developed we are, we will have personal needs that sometimes require us to put ourselves first. Taking care of ourselves doesn't mean we're not operating from unconditional love; it just means we love ourselves as unconditionally as we love others. As we "transcend and include", we still need to attend to our own more primal needs.

Because we're no longer getting triggered and stuck in old emotional patterns, we are liberated to be our unique emotional self. At this point you find yourself permitting your emotions to be what they are, even though your feelings may be completely different from everybody else's – or even your own, just moments earlier. You could be in a situation where everybody is crying and you're laughing; some old part of you may be concerned about this, but at this point you simply have to be who you are, while also being aware of and sensitive to your impact on others.

One of the wonderful benefits of having worked through 80% or more of the emotional issues in Stage 10 is that it leaves us much more willing to be vulnerable with others. This results in much deeper, more connective, and more fulfilling relationships. We also become far less attached to avoiding things we don't like. We realize that real connection with others requires us to be willing to feel and be impacted by our own truth and others' truths, no matter how painful that may be, without reacting, defending, or avoiding. The real test is our willingness to hear and feel the other's perspective and allow ourselves to be truly changed by it, as appropriate. When we're done saying, "I won't let anyone change me," then we are able to grow faster than ever.

Thomas: I used to have a lot of romantic ideas about unconditional love, so it took me awhile to notice when it was happening for me. I found myself wanting the best for myself and everyone around me, even when people would cut me off on the highway. It wasn't coming from an ideal; it's just that I could see myself in everyone. I felt love for everyone, whether they appeared to deserve it or not.

- Journal: What still holds me back from crying? What holds me back from feeling or expressing anger? Sadness? Joy? Disappointment? Failure?
- Do things that express your love for others. It can be small things, like sending a note, or telling someone what they mean to you. The old habits of withholding our expressions of love will change as we practice letting our love flow into the world through our thoughts, speech, and action.

Stage 11 - Body

Location Description: Moving from body's unconditioned wisdom

Needs: To discover how to move in alignment with self

"The body never lies." – Martha Graham

Once we move from the transforming space of Stage 10 into the individuating energy of Stage 11, we can feel the immense wisdom of our body and we are much freer to live our natural way of being in the world. At this point, following the prompts of the body is important and necessary in order to live our deepest potential.

The body is now quite open and transparent, operating in alignment with our natural personality. What we think and feel, our body enacts and embodies. This doesn't mean we don't care about our impact on others; it means we care about others *while* doing what is authentic for us to do, informed by our unified connection with everything and everyone. At this point, we have not only realized the unity between self and others, but we are truly living and embodying that realization.

In the Dual Phase, when we felt more fractured, we may have experienced things going wrong when trusting our body. But at this stage, we are much more deeply aware of and aligned with ourselves, and we're much more deeply healed and integrated. At this stage, trusting our body and allowing it to lead becomes paramount.

Mark: These days, I feel deeply present in my body. Even when I'm at work, I feel my body no matter what's happening. I've learned to follow my body all the time and stop doubting it. I'm no longer watching over my body like a critical parent. I'm just letting it be.

- Journal: What prevents me from following my body's spontaneous prompts?
- Practice allowing your body to choose what to do next. Go for a walk, ignore your mind for a little while, and follow what your body prefers. You may be surprised at the wisdom of the body's impulses at this stage.

Stage 12: Living Potential

Stage Overview: Serving from alignment of purpose and power

- Subjective: Serving the world by giving deepest gifts
- Observable: Displays trust in being and doing
- Relational: Generously sharing from deepest essence
- Systemic: Fully liberated to give one's gifts to systems

Needs: To bring my unique gifts into the world

Identity: I am everything, passionately giving my deepest gifts

"Through your awakening, you awaken others."
— Solara An Ra

As we enter Stage 12, we experience living our unique gifts without self-negation. At this point, we are living in deep trust of ourselves and deep trust in being. We allow ourselves to impact others in a bigger way than ever before. The universe will prompt you to use your gifts to help others in ways you could not have conceived from the perspective of your individual existence.

Toward the end of Stage 12, questions about the meaning of surrender become huge. The universe will shake you again and again, as if to say "are you really ready to surrender – even to this?" This does not mean you need to give up your sense of what is right or what you should do. It only means you are being asked to give up resistance to all of what is, including how you're showing up.

At this stage, you will be challenged with everything you wish you could control... until you realize that you can't control life, resistance is futile, and you'll never win an argument with reality. Through this process, you'll discover your own brand of faith, including a deep knowing that no matter what happens, everything is perfect. Toward the end of Stage 12, life will challenge you to fully release your separate sense of self into the mystery and fully trust in Being.

Justin: I was really scared to come out as a writer. I was so sure I'd be rejected. But actually, I've found a lot of acceptance. At this point, I'm working on my third book, and there's nothing left in me that stops at the old fears. I'm just doing my thing, and I never hold myself back.

- Journal: If you had unlimited resources, what would you do?
- Whatever your answer above, start doing that now. Don't wait for anything, including money. Trust that the universe will support your efforts.

Stage 12 - Consciousness

Location Description: Serving from fully engaged presence

Needs: To bring your full presence into everything you do

"This is the real secret of life – to be completely engaged with what you are doing in the here and now." –Alan Watts

In Stage 12, we are fully engaged with living our purpose. The old fears of the consequences of living our truth don't stop us anymore. Our awareness is fully and deeply present in what we are doing. At the same time, consciousness is so released into what's happening that even our old desire to identify our sense of self with consciousness begins to dissolve.

Zoe: I'm finding that in my therapy practice, most of what really helps my clients is my total presence with them. Even when I'm having a bad day, I can put all that aside and be totally there. When my day is over, I can instantly switch to my personal life with my family. I never imagined I could be so present like that.

- Practice staying deeply present with yourself when you feel pressured or uncomfortable.
- Practice being deeply present with someone who is experiencing pain or discomfort.

Stage 12 - Uniqueness

Location Description: Serving by living deepest purpose

Needs: To live your deepest purpose despite fears of consequences

*"Trusting your individual uniqueness challenges you
to lay yourself open." – James Broughton*

In Stage 12 we are deeply liberated from our conditioning and we find ourselves living our unique truth. We are able to serve from our deepest purpose. At this point all the fears that we had about sharing who we really are simply don't matter. You're either going to be who you are or get sick from trying to avoid it. At this stage, you become sick of holding yourself back and have no option but to manifest your purpose.

You may wonder 'What might happen if I fully come out and live my truth in the world?' Maybe some people you care about won't like you. Maybe some will reject or misunderstand you. But at this point, those fearful voices are not what's running the show. At this stage, you can't NOT express your full uniqueness, whatever that looks like, and whatever might happen in that process. After a while, you'll notice that expressing your true uniqueness is far more fulfilling than waiting until it feels safe to be who you are. The relaxation of this realization helps move you into the Singular Phase.

Sam: My whole life I yearned to feel like I was giving my deepest gifts. But I don't yearn for that anymore. I'm just doing it.

- Journal: Do I have any remaining resistance to doing what I'm here to do or be?
- Take action; do something that expresses your purpose whether you are being paid to or not.

Stage 12 - Mind

Location Description: Serving life through potent clarity

Needs: To think and express authenticity despite fears of consequences

"You are here in order to enable the world to live more amply, with greater vision, with a finer spirit of hope and achievement. You are here to enrich the world, and you impoverish yourself if you forget the errand."
– Woodrow Wilson

Having individuated in Stage 11, we find ourselves in Stage 12 challenged to bring our own unique thoughts and ways of communicating them into the world, despite our own biggest fears about what that might bring. Galileo is a perfect example of this; knowing that the church considered heretical his idea that the earth is not the center of the universe, he spoke his truth anyway and paid for it with imprisonment. But Galileo knew he would live in a prison of his own making if he didn't speak his truth. It didn't take long before his unique way of thinking sparked a complete revolution in astronomy and astrophysics. At Stage 12, each of us is required to speak and live our truth or imprison ourselves by holding our ideas back. Trust that no matter what happens, you will fulfill your purpose by bringing your unique ideas and visions into the world.

Helena: At some point, I stopped caring about awakening myself. My entire focus is on helping others to awaken. I have my own vision of how to accomplish that, and that's what my life is about.

- Write or create something that expresses your unique beliefs and post it somewhere on the internet where others can see it and respond.
- Convince at least one other person to support your unique beliefs in a tangible way.

Stage 12 - Emotions

Location Description: Serving from unconditional love

Needs: To emote authentically despite fears of consequences

"Be true to your heart... put your whole heart and soul into it, and then whatever you do, it will shine through."
– Jamie Brewer

At Stage 12, we experience a flow of love and gratitude and a connectedness with all of life. We automatically give our love in ways that empower others to be who they are. We bring deep, compassionate emotional presence to our work and relationships.

At first, expressing your emotional truth can feel like agony. It can feel quite vulnerable exposing your true feelings, especially when others are not doing the same. But the need to serve others by feeling and expressing your true emotions wins over fear. The need to serve in an open-hearted way becomes your new reality.

Vicky: Looking back at my past, I can see that I never really did anything "wholeheartedly" – there was always a part of me that questioned myself and held myself back. But that's over. Everything I do now I do with my whole heart and my whole being.

- Empower someone who looks up to you. Help them feel safe and encourage them to express their true feelings no matter what the consequences may be for you.
- Is there something you don't feel grateful for? Journal about why.

Stage 12 - Body

Location Description: Serving from deeply embodied presence

Needs: To act from authenticity despite fears of consequences

"If you're not living your truth, you're living a lie."
— Joseph Curiale

At Stage 12, we are compelled to serve others by physically enacting our truth in the world. All the fears of what might happen if we embody our truth become secondary; all that matters is manifesting our deepest essence through our physical form.

Later in Stage 12, we're at the edge of the Singular Realization in Phase 3. On the physical level, any last traces of resistance to who we are in the world, how our body wants to function, or how we naturally want to relate with others will be transcended here. Once we have learned to completely trust our body to express in its own natural way, we can relax and allow our body's innate wisdom to lead the way.

David: I felt as if a dam had burst, and everything inside of me flooded out into the world in hundreds of very specific ways through dozens of projects. All the previous withholding was over. It was time to manifest my personal destiny no matter how challenging that was.

- Find something your body has always wanted to do and do it.
- Volunteer to do something tangible for others that represents who you are.

Section 5:
Developing in the Singular Phase

*"When you lose all sense of yourself, the bonds of
a thousand chains will vanish." – Rumi*

As the Singular Phase dawns, there is a remarkable
dissolution of what previously was felt as a subject/object
perspective. That is, we felt we were a subject here, having
an experience with people and things over there. Even in
the Unified Phase, there was always a "me" and an "other".

But the shift into Singular Realization removes the "me" from that perspective, leaving only what is.

This experience of seamless non-separation, or what some call "non-duality", starts by removing your sense of self from the center of your own being. For others, a better description is that the awareness of 'what is' becomes far more dominant than the awareness of all previous senses of self, including, and especially, the awakened ones. You discover that your life is far freer and more impactful without a sense of separate self getting in the way.

Wisdom is a word that describes life in Phase 3. At this point in our development, we have travelled the journey from Dual, to Unified, to Singular. We went from seeking ourselves, to finding ourselves, to transcending and including all of ourselves. We have the wisdom to understand the journey of others, and we have gotten out of our own way enough to truly be there for others in the ways they uniquely need. We have also unleashed our unique creativity, freeing ourselves to bring forth our unique gifts.

Please note that we are not specifying needs in the Singular Phase because we are no longer primarily driven by needs that feel personal. It's not that we have no more personal needs, but at this point what drives most people is fulfilling our purpose through service to others. Likewise, we are not including practices in the Singular Phase. This is because there is no separate sense of self remaining that would want to practice for the sake of growing oneself. At this Stage, it's obvious that we are part of universal evolution, doing whatever life prompts and growing spontaneously.

Stage 13: Singular Realization

Stage Overview: Dissolution of subject/object perspective

- Subjective: Life spontaneously unfolding
- Observable: Exhibits nonresistance to life's fluctuations
- Relational: Nonresistance to fluctuations in relating
- Systemic: Nonresistance to fluctuations in systems

"The personal life deeply lived always expands into truths beyond itself." –Anais Nin

We call Stage 13 Singular Realization because once we've let go of our last resistance to life and our unnecessary forms of control, something extraordinary happens. We experience a shift unlike anything before. The subject/object structure that shaped all our previous experience dissolves, leaving nothing in its wake that is recognizable as a self, at least in the old sense. Certainly not the glorious holistic unified self that we experienced in the prior 4 stages; even that identity has evaporated, leaving only a sense of infinite mystery.

In Stage 13, the meaning of getting out of your own way is made clear; you are no longer inserting yourself between stimulus and response. There is no longer a separate "you" who could even want to interfere with yourself or your natural responses. You are simply the dance of life. Unlike the Phase 2 realization which is about an awakened and unified sense of self, the shift into Singular Realization is not about self at all. If anything, it's about selflessness. This is not to say that we no longer exist, because we do. It's just that our actions are guided by mystery, and whatever self-sense remains is dwarfed by the play of life.

It's important that we explain what we mean by "non-resistance" at this stage. It's not that we don't have any desire to move against anything, it's that we have no impulse to move against our own natural reactions. If someone comes at us with an energy we don't like, we may naturally resist. But in Stage 13, there is no inner resistance to the impulse to resist.

It turns out that fear of full immersion in life was the last thing creating an illusory separation. Having surrendered our sense of separate self, we are free to fully participate in each moment, no matter how much we love or hate it. We still have our preferences and we still want to change things, but we're not resisting the fact that the universe keeps giving us assignments that take us out of our comfort zone. This makes us reliable agents of being, serving in whatever ways are most needed. This is no longer an idea; it's simply what is.

This stage is also about the surrender of the need for self-referencing. We are deeply conditioned to turn our attention to ourselves to "check in", to make sure our self is ok. But after crossing into Stage 13, there is no further need for that. With no self-referencing, we stop the lifelong habit of recreating a separate self-sense. When that activity is subtracted from our life, all that remains is the endless dance of action and experience.

In some ways, Singular Realization is far too simple to comprehend. It's not about you experiencing what is, it's simply what is. At the core is the recognition of having passed beyond surrender. The word surrender itself suggests a self surrendering to another. But as the Singular Realization dawns, the old subject/object perspective vanishes, leaving nothing but mystery in motion. Some describe this as "beyond the beyond".

Emma: One day I woke up and I was gone. What a relief! It's not like there's nothing left of "me", it's just that I have no impulse to reflect on myself as a separate person anymore. It's very hard to describe, but it's incredibly liberating.

Stage 13 - Consciousness

Location Description: Awareness released from self-referencing

"I turned my gaze inward and what I saw stopped me in my tracks. Instead of the usual unlocalized center of myself, there was nothing there, it was empty, and at the moment of seeing this there was a flood of quiet joy and I knew what was missing - it was my 'self'." – Bernadette Roberts

Experience in Stage 13 happens without subject/object duality. The notion of self as consciousness, Unity, or Everything is gone. By "awareness released from self-referencing", we mean that the lifelong habit of turning our attention back to self has ceased. What remains is only what is happening. We are completely given over to what we are here to be and do.

Daniel: At first, I felt like I was being replaced by life. Later, I could look back and see that without even knowing it, I had released a need for a separate individual self. It's not that I stopped being me, it's that my need for a sense of self had simply gone away. Even the awakened sense of self I had through my unity realization was gone. I started to recognize that this shift wasn't about me; it was about Life.

Stage 13 - Uniqueness

Location Description: Personality expresses without attachment to sense of self

"Everyone has a purpose in life and a unique talent to give to others. When we blend this unique talent with service to others, we experience the ecstasy and exultation of the spirit, which is the ultimate goal of all goals." – Kallam Anji Reddy

At this point, there is no more fighting for or against your own or anyone else's uniqueness. Your unique personality is part of the seamless dance of life. The resistance inherent in subject/object perspective is gone. The flavors of our uniqueness are released into life, guided by mystery.

Claire: I used to have a strong sense of self attached to my personality, so I was astonished to see that my personality didn't actually need "me"! Since experiencing a shift recently, my personality goes on, but I wouldn't even know how to turn that into a sense of self anymore.

Stage 13 - Mind

Location Description: Thoughts happen without attachment to sense of self

"When you've seen beyond yourself, then you may find, peace of mind is waiting there." – George Harrison

In Stage 13, there is no longer confusion or conflict about who or what is the author of our thoughts. Thoughts are just happening, there's no concern about whether they are my thoughts or the universe's thoughts. Thoughts are simply waves of intelligence that move through us without resistance; they are part of how the universe lives us.

Aaron: My mind no longer frets about future or past. There are only practical thoughts and actions. This way of being feels way simpler.

Stage 13 - Emotions

Location Description: Emotions happen without attachment to sense of self

"To be awake on the level of emotion means to no longer be deriving a sense of self from how and what we feel."
– Adyashanti

Prior to the Singular Phase, difficult feelings arose as life was pushing you to open your heart and live out loud. But by Stage 13, life's difficulties present no obstacle. What really pushes you over the line from Unified to Singular is that you're done trying to control how you feel and how life feels, leaving you in simple presence.

In the Unified Phase, you realized that you are life. In the Singular Phase, you realize that life is living you. You find yourself spontaneously on the ride: you're laughing, you're crying, you're scared, you're feeling in awe. All of these things flow in and out without any resistance at all.

Gratitude is something we all experience at times in our lives when we feel supported, appreciated, empowered, or abundant. But that level of gratitude comes and goes. In Stage 13 a form of gratitude dawns that is unshakeable.

Wendy: Love and emotions are waves; I no longer experience a "me" in that. Life is just happening.

Stage 13 - Body

Location Description: Body moves without attachment to sense of self

"Life is the dancer and you are the dance." – Eckart Tolle

Prior to Stage 13, a division was held between body and other Domains, or between body and world. Even in the Unified Phase, there was a subtle holding of separation. But starting in Phase 3, all such perception is gone. There are distinctions, but no separation. We find ourselves in the physical dance of life without resistance.

Rene: I felt released from all attempts to manage my body any more than it wanted to be managed. That put me into a space of remarkable transparency. It was as if I could see through the world... not with these eyes, but through the fundamental knowingness that everything is simultaneously transparent and apparently solid.

Stage 14: Flow

Stage Overview: Life in fluid motion

- Subjective: Life in frictionless flow
- Observable: Seemingly unstoppable flow
- Relational: Continuous flow in relationships
- Systemic: Contributes continuous flow in systems

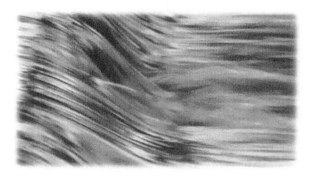

"You are a function of what the whole universe is doing in the same way that a wave is a function of what the whole ocean is doing." – Alan Watts

We call Stage 14 Flow because at this point non-resistance turns to fluid motion. Even when life brings you staccato rhythms, you are flowing freely with it. It doesn't mean you like everything or that life is always bliss. It means you are beyond resistance to the point of knowing that all experiences are part of the flow of life. Whatever challenge life throws at you, your response is part of the flow.

This is far beyond saying yes to everything life brings, because saying yes would mean you'd have to stop long enough to consider whether to say yes or no. This is living in surrender beyond the possibility of deciding yes or no. It's like being consciously swept down the river of life without resistance. Choices are happening in every moment, but even those are simply part of the motion of the river.

Nathan: I had no idea what flow was until flow became everything I experience.

Stage 14 - Consciousness

Location Description: Awareness flows without resistance

*"Let things flow naturally forward
in whatever way they like." – Lao Tzu*

In Stage 14, it's hard to think of this Domain as consciousness anymore; there is only the flow of life. The awareness that previously seemed transcendent is known simply an aspect of totality. Consciousness no longer appears beyond the material level of existence because everything is known as part of everything.

Sara: It's become obvious that what I used to think of as consciousness is just part of what Life is.

Stage 14 - Uniqueness

Location Description: Free flowing personality

"If you know what makes you happy, your personality, interests and capabilities, just use them, and everything else flows beautifully." – Juhi Chawla

At Stage 13, we experience our personality flowing freely in the world without internal resistance. There is nothing left of ourselves that would stop or resist that flow. Being your deepest, most authentic self turns out to feel like a selfless flow of the flavor you impart to the world.

Alex: It's really amazing how much my sense of myself was preventing me from being me. Now there is only the flow of giving my gifts.

Stage 14 - Mind

Location Description: Freely-flowing intelligence

"Everything in the universe has a purpose. Indeed, the invisible intelligence that flows through everything in a purposeful fashion is also flowing through you." – Wayne Dyer

At this point we find ourselves on the ride of life without resistance to our own or others' thoughts or beliefs. This doesn't mean we don't care about thoughts or beliefs, only that we have no attachment to how intelligence flows through us. We experience mind as another frequency in the flow. Mental realities move through us, and we are simply playing our part in the bigger picture.

Ava: It's obvious that the intelligence that flows through everything flows through me. I'm released from needing any of that to be about me.

Stage 14 – Emotions

Location Description: Love in continuous flow

"Let love flow so that it cleanses the world." – Sai Baba

Stage 14 in the Emotions Domain can be described as love in fluid motion. Love has many flavors; it can feel big, soft, and connected. It can also feel like a sword, cutting away what is not true or life-supporting. Love can feel strong just as much as tender and vulnerable. At this point, all forms of love and feelings flow through us without restriction or attachment to a sense of self.

Ron: It's not that everything in my life is perfect, and it's not that I'm happy all the time. I just feel Life as a river of love.

Stage 14 - Body

Location Description: Body flows freely through world

*"Once we open up to the flow of energy within our body,
we can also open up to the flow of energy in the universe."*
– Wilhelm Reich

The experience here is of a seamless flow of the universe flowing through our body, and our body flowing through the world. Even when our body feels stressed or tired, there is no resistance to that. There is only action in alignment with our natural purpose and function.

Samir: At first, I realized I was simply a part of the dance of life. Then that realization went deep enough that the dominant experience was a feeling of being in free flow on all levels, including physically. Living in this place has been something I never imagined was possible.

Ruby: I've always loved to dance and move my body. But now I'm seeing that my whole life is a dance, and I can move from that same place I do when I'm dancing. It feels like life is dancing through me.

Stage 15: Unknown

Stage Overview: Ongoing evolution

The purpose of putting "Unknown" at Stage 15 on our model is to underscore the point that there is no end to human evolution. Just as there is no end to evolution in the universe, it seems to us that there is no such thing as a "highest" or "most developed" stage. As long as humans exist, we believe everyone will experience a continuous journey of development. We will continue to collect data about higher stages of development, and when we can see more clearly what Stage 15 is about, we'll add that and promote "Unknown" to Stage 16.

"The mystery of life isn't a problem to solve, but a reality to experience." – Frank Herbert

What Stage 15 might look like is hard to predict, but it seems clear that socially interconnected technologies will be part of it. We expect to see technologies increasingly devoted to human evolution through integrations with artificial intelligence. We think such synergies will enable awakenings to happen not just in individuals, but in groups.

Conclusion

In this book, we have tried to describe what we see as the universal human journey from apparent separateness to awakened unity and beyond. We evolve from feeling fractured to knowing that all of life is one thing, living through us with infinite love and intelligence. We grow from not knowing who we are or what we are doing here, to knowing ourselves deeply and fulfilling our unique purpose. We learn to live so deeply aligned with self and life that we are surrendered into mystery, with flow as the central feature of our experience.

Please remember that your personal journey of unfoldment is not likely to completely align with the order in which we're presented our stages. Our model merely depicts the averages we've seen and what experts we've reviewed have written about. The way it happens for you is what really matters.

It's hard to overstate the importance of accelerating this journey for our own wellness and the wellness of humanity. In our opinion, unfolding our deepest potential is no longer an optional endeavor. We have precious few years in which to awaken our deepest capacities, save our planet from human devastation, and learn to live in collective, co-creative unity. We believe that living from our deepest capacity is key to fundamental wellness and thriving for all beings. We hope we have inspired you to find your own path to this type of deeply embodied awakeness.

We encourage you to sign up for a free account at iConscious. global, take our assessment, and get a custom results report to understand how to most directly accelerate your evolution. On our site, you can also get access resources and stay informed through our free newsletter. We also offer professional coaching sessions for those interested in accelerating their development, as well as coach and leader certification courses for those interested in assisting others in their awakening process.

We hope this book gave you a clear understanding of the vast potential you can live — for your own fulfillment as well as for others. May you live your deepest potential and inspire others to do the same!

Section 6: Appendix

Carole's Story

Growing up, as far back as I can remember, I had a deep curiosity about life .. for what is really going on, what is reality, what is the purpose of all this, what is really true, and why are we all even here. I was raised in a small metaphysical religion that provided insights and experiences into the insubstantiality of the physical realm, the power of thought, and unconditional love as an intangible, ever-presence that's everywhere. This foundation satiated many of my questions, and yet left me with just as many unanswered. I felt I had a partial picture, but not a complete, whole understanding. I felt a constant light thread of anxiety; something was missing.

After college, I graduated with a bachelors degree along with much confusion and uncertainty of what I was meant to do or be in this world. I had a deep and persistent gnawing that something wasn't quite right; something was lacking. This led me on a deep search, which for me, felt like an insatiable quest for deeper and more satisfying answers. I yearned to feel complete, content, and okay. I wanted to know the "truth" of this life, which led me to become what I like to call a "professional seeker." For the next 15 years, I went on dozens of long, silent meditation retreats, followed gurus and satsang meetings all over the world, attended many, many workshops locally and internationally, worked with various therapists for several years as well as a life coach I talked to regularly, and read every book possible about freedom, human potential, psychology, leadership, enlightenment, and anything that promised to 'discover who I am' and what was fundamentally real. I was all over the place! .. on an unstoppable mission in search for answers, for clarity, for understanding... for myself, of myself. Through all of this, I was attempting to fill/complete myself in many different ways, which showed up and manifested differently depending on the stage of development I was in at the time.

Along my search, consciousness began to awaken to itself. I realized I was consciousness itself; not my thoughts, feelings, or body (as they say in Sanskrit, "neti neti", which means, "not this, not that"). I realized that who I was was not confined to the appearing boundaries of my skin. I, consciousness, didn't start and stop within the walls of the skin. "I" was everywhere! This felt incredibly freeing and opening, and provided huge relief and liberation from feeling confined and limited from an old, small sense of self. And for once, I felt contentment, I felt here, whole, and happy! The nagging need and desire to search was gone. I found what I was looking for; which was nothing more than myself/awakened consciousness. I/this was fully here all along! Ha! It was me searching for myself! "What you are looking for is what is looking."

This deep contentment lasted about six months, and then the seeking came back; something was missing again. Although free in one respect, I felt detached and separate from life, like I couldn't fully feel or relate to all of what was here. So, back to the familiar searching bandwagon, I stumbled upon Waking Down in Mutuality (WDM). WDM showed me a big piece I was missing: not just waking up to consciousness, but "waking down"/dropping fully into my heart and body. This led me/consciousness straight down and into my body, rather than just up and out and transcending the physical body, thoughts, emotions, etc. I realized I wasn't just consciousness, I am this body, thoughts, and emotions. I was completely bypassing half of life by exclusively identifying with consciousness (which was part of the process to un-attach and then fully include) and dividing and ignoring everything else (mostly that which was uncomfortable). No wonder I felt incomplete with something missing! I didn't want to feel all the division, discomfort, and unmet trauma that was still frozen in my body just waiting to be fully seen and integrated. And yet the very avoidance of feeling divided was the division itself!

It became really clear that it wasn't enough to wake up to consciousness and transcend all of what I didn't want to see. Waking up to/as consciousness itself was just the beginning. Consciousness was waking up ALL unconscious, divided, and remaining areas throughout the rest of my body; anything unmet (psychologically) or stuck was being illuminated like a bright flashlight as it dropped down through my entire system. Any shadows or beliefs and emotions not yet seen and loved as a part of me were up to be fully acknowledged, met, and fully included. No stone left unturned. Consciousness descended through my system and landed like a spaceship at the base of my feet. I felt here; fully here, in my body - yet everywhere - with my body in me. I was fully alive for the first time, needing absolutely nothing. This brought a sense of deep completeness, wholeness, vast-spaciousness, and loving, heart-opening, connection as unconditional love. I felt a clear sense of unity, oneness with/as everything.

This deep embodiment provided the perfect container for remaining triggers and unmet traumas to come to the surface, to become conscious, and thus no longer unconsciously drive my behavior, decisions, and perspective on self, others, and life (which they do, until we become aware). Every part of me was waking up — including my uniqueness/purpose, emotions and heart, mind and thinking, and my body. Each of these domains of my being had a different, and important, flavor of awakening.

During those years searching, I completed my Masters degree and decided to pursue and complete my Doctorate degree in Professional Coaching and Human Development. I had already been coaching people in the realm of health and wellness and loved working with individuals 1:1. I wanted to go deeper. I wanted to broaden and extend what I was offering in my current coaching practice to include the research and science – and the art of it's application (coaching) – of human development, the evolution of consciousness, people/ leadership development, and all of what I was experiencing and discovering in recognizing my inherent freedom and living my full purpose and potential on my own journey.

Through my years as a professional coach, I noticed a dramatic difference in how people transformed; clearly influenced by where I was on my own journey and the lens I was peering through in how I saw and defined myself, them, and the world. "Self as instrument" became obvious; it wasn't so much the particular tools I was using (although still very useful), but what/how I was seeing/identifying myself and them that had immeasurable impact. This led me to research and write my PhD dissertation on how the coach identifies him/herself and the immense impact that has on the transformational possibilities of the client. I published this as a book, *Space to See Reality: A new model for professional coaches,* and began working more and more with high impact leaders and executives in various companies all over the world. I realized that if every individual IS the actual instrument for change in the world (how awake - in all domains - are the leaders running companies, cities, countries, and our future), it's best to start at the top with those high impact people and structure/policy makers and the conscious impact will trickle down and through. The level of development we each operate at is exactly what we create and exponentially put out in the world. Our level of development IS making the all the decisions, and for CEO's, it's deciding the direction of the entire company. If what's being created comes from individual and collective levels of development/consciousness, it seemed like a perfect acupuncture point (along with AI – more about this on my website) to work with to create the greatest possibility of change in the world.

The more I coached with leaders at various companies, the more I realized that people really needed a map of where they are and where they're going. I realized during my search that there wasn't a path or a map to help me understand where I was in my developmental process and where I was headed. Without a map, I took many, many detours and hit many unnecessary dead ends along the way. Through my research on human development, it became apparent that there were many partial models out there claiming to be the full 'human development' picture. Yet almost all of the models were very partial. Some just included the development and evolution of consciousness, some just emotional intelligence, some just on the subjective experience and not relational, some just the physical age and development of a physical human over time, and almost all of them stopped at Stage 6, of which I knew there were more stages beyond that. I wanted a model that showed it all; a framework that showed all domains and all stages – even beyond what was currently written about. This was the start of the iConscious Human Development Model, and is the foundation for the assessment and all courses and consulting we offer.

The model not only gave me a framework to use as a coach, but it gave my clients a framework to really grok what this whole process looked like, all the pieces involved, and how to go about leaning into the parts that were relatively unmet and not yet integrated. Between the research in all the current maps and models on human development and consciousness evolution, my colleague and cofounder Ted, and I were able to synthesize all (as much as we could find) the content currently completed, expand it to include parts that have previously been left out, and further elucidate development that was yet to be clearly written about (everything post Stage 6). This is what has brought us to where we are today.

Ted's Story

As a child, I was fascinated by the observation that most people around me (both at home and in school) seemed mysteriously perturbed in ways no one was talking about. Something felt wrong and hidden in a way I couldn't grasp. But I wanted to. I wanted to understand myself, people, and the world.

In grammar school, my teachers regarded me as smart, but not using my full potential. I had no idea what it would mean to use my full potential because nobody ever talked about that. As I grew, my questions about life, the human condition, and what my potential might be only increased. I wasn't finding satisfying answers, so one day I asked the rabbi "What is the meaning of life?" "Life," said the rabbi, "is a mystery." I took that to mean he also didn't have the answers, so I decided to go figure out life for myself.

At age 13 I began reading eastern philosophy books and taking personal development seminars. I was also taking initiations into esoteric practices that promised to expand my awareness. I soon realized that the one thing I could do to help make the world better was to help people realize their full potential. It was obvious that the destructive potentials of our technology were evolving as quickly as the creative potentials, and our only hope of survival is for as many people as possible to become deeply awake and connected. That appears to be even more true today. But it was also clear that I had to find awakening for myself before

I could help others.

At 17, I began to practice Transcendental Meditation, and after several years of training, I started working with students. After 10 years I noticed that I had plenty of expanded experiences, but I still didn't feel fundamentally awake in consciousness or very developed in my emotions or relationships. In fact, I was still unclear about who I was, why I was here, or what it even means to be human. This realization propelled me into years of deeper searching and practice through numerous schools of personal, spiritual, and relational development.

Finally, starting around age 40, I experienced a major consciousness awakening (Stage 7). I realized I was the infinite spaciousness that experienced all my thoughts, feelings and sensations. I thought I'd become enlightened, until I realized this was just the start. I saw that I wasn't really in my body and that I was rejecting big parts of myself by avoiding all manner of discomforts. But at this point, I was ready to lean in and claim all of my reality.

Through this exploration, I discovered what I wondered as a child was so perturbing to most people: the underlying angst of being a simultaneously limitless and limited creature. It became clear through my own process that most people are not aware of this feeling for several reasons. First, most are too busy focusing on everyday work and issues; too busy to notice something that can be subtle and elusive. Second, even when that level of angst is encountered, we tend to think it means there's something wrong with us or with the world, so we often use our energy and attention trying to fix it. And even when we're not trying to fix it, we are all so conditioned to avoid discomfort that we almost instinctively turn our attention to things that feel more comfortable.

Fortunately, I learned to simply embrace this angst in myself, not to make it go away, but to claim it as part of who I am. This decision instantly triggered a profound transformation that dropped me into my body and opened me to the unity of life (Stage 9). It turned out that I'd been perpetuating my own internal split by rejecting pain. This shift radically and permanently changed my perspective and eventually brought me to a deep and abiding wellness. I finally realized the meaning of life: It's a mystery! Turned out the rabbi was right. But it was clearly my destiny to undertake my own journey so I could articulate it for others in ways that help them awaken more directly.

The shifts I experienced from that time forward inspired me to help others find that same deep well-being for themselves. I then spent 19 years building the foundations in a form of work called Waking Down, designing and presenting core dharma workshops along with mentor and teacher training programs. Starting in 1998, I worked in depth with thousands of students to assist their process of growing and awakening into fundamental wellness and wholeness. I also experimented with many ways of mapping personal development. Through this experience, I discovered ways to streamline awakening and maturation, enabling most aspirants to experience major shifts in days or months instead of years or lifetimes.

Looking back on the twisted path of my own development, it's obvious that if I had a clear map of the process, I could easily have unfolded my potential in a far shorter time – and for a lot less money! By the time I was 40, I had spent about 27 years and over $350,000 (in today's money) to explore myself and life before I was able to awaken to unity. Yet soon after that, I was able to help hundreds into that same stage of development, usually in a matter of weeks or months. This confirmed for me that human development can easily move far faster than anyone had previously suggested.

My continuing explorations of my own and my clients' development began to reveal further stages of development that were not commonly known or articulated at the time. It began to emerge that the unity shift was nothing like an end to development, and in fact presented itself as a new beginning. For years after that shift, I went through a long series of enormous healings that shook me to my core, bringing my realized oneness into deep embodiment and integration. It forced me to go beyond self-realization into healing my relationships, activating my deeper purpose, empowering devoted service to others, and enabling many forms of fulfillment.

By 2014, it was clear that to accomplish my mission of helping the planet awaken quickly, a realistic high-resolution model was needed as a basis for all future coaching work, online education, and transformation through artificial agents. That's when I met Carole and we began this work.

Footnotes

[1]Heffernan, M., Quinn Griffin, M. T., McNulty, S. R., & Fitzpatrick, J. J. (2010). Self-compassion and emotional intelligence in nurses. International journal of nursing practice, 16(4), 366-373; Homan, K. J. (2016). Self-compassion and psychological well-being in older adults. Journal ofAdult Development, 23(2), 111-119; Jennings, P. A., & Greenberg, M. T. (2009). The Prosocial Classroom: Teacher Social and Emotional Competence in Relation to Student and Classroom Outcomes. Review of Educational Research, 79(1), 491-525.

[2]Bonini, A. N. (2008). Cross-national variation in individual life satisfaction: Effects of national wealth, human development, and environmental conditions. Social indicators research, 87(2), 223-236; Welzel, C., & Inglehart, R. (2010). Agency, values, and well-being: A human development model. Social indicators research, 97(1), 43-63.

[3]Ull.n, F., de Manzano, .., Almeida, R., Magnusson, P. K., Pedersen, N. L., Nakamura, J., Madison, G. (2012). Proneness for psychological flow in everyday life: Associations with personality and intelligence. Personality and Individual Differences, 52(2), 167-172; Aub., C., Brunelle, E., & Rousseau, V. (2014). Flow experience and team performance: The role of team goal commitment and information exchange. Motivation and Emotion, 38(1), 120-130.

[4]Currie, J. (2009). Healthy, wealthy, and wise: Socioeconomic status, poor health in childhood, and human capital

development. Journal of Economic Literature, 47(1), 87-122; Morisaki, N., Togoobaatar, G., Vogel, J., Souza, J., Rowland Hogue, C., Jayaratne, K., Network, N. H. R. (2014). Risk factors for spontaneous and provider-initiated preterm deliveryin high and low Human Development Index countries: a secondary analysis of the World Health Organization Multicountry Survey on Maternal and Newborn Health. BJOG: An International Journal of Obstetrics & Gynaecology, 121, 101-109; Khazaei, S., Armanmehr, V., Nematollahi, S., Rezaeian, S., &Khazaei, S. (2017). Suicide rate in relation to the Human Development Index and other health related factors: A global ecological study from 91 countries. Journal of Epidemiology and Global Health, 7(2), 131-134; Schimmel, J. (2009). Development as happiness: The subjective perception of happiness andUNDP's analysis of poverty, wealth and development. Journal of Happiness Studies, 10(1), 93-111; Minas, H. (2013). Human Security, Complexity, and Mental Health System Development. Global Mental Health: Principles and Practice, 48.

[5]Singh, G. K., Azuine, R. E., &Siahpush, M. (2012). Global inequalities in cervical cancer incidence and mortality are linked to deprivation, low socioeconomic status, and human development. International Journal of MCH and AIDS, 1(1), 17; Alvarez, J. L., Gil, R., Hern.ndez, V., & Gil, A. (2009). Factors associated with maternal mortality in Sub-Saharan Africa: an ecological study. BMC public health, 9(1), 462.

[6]Momeni, N. (2009). The relation between managers' emotional intelligence and the organizational climate

they create. Public Personnel Management, 38(2), 35-48; Stubbs Koman, E., & Wolff, S. B. (2008). Emotional intelligence competencies in the team and team leader: A multi-level examination of the impact of emotional intelligence on team performance. Journal of Management Development, 27(1), 55-75.

[7]Kidwell, B., Hardesty, D. M., Murtha, B. R., & Sheng, S. (2011). Emotional intelligence in marketing exchanges. .Journal of Marketing, 75(1), 78-95; Thirumurthy, H., Galarraga, O., Larson, B., & Rosen, S. (2012). HIV treatment produces economic returns through increased work and education, and warrants continued US support. Health Affairs, 31(7), 1470-1477;

[8]Sušnik, J., & van der Zaag, P. (2017). Correlation and causation between the UN HumanDevelopment Index and national and personal wealth and resource exploitation. Economic Research-Ekonoms kalstraživanja, 30(1), 1705-1723; McKee, M., Suhrcke, M., Nolte, E., Lessof, S., Figueras, J., Duran, A., &Menabde, N. (2009). Health systems, health, and wealth: a European perspective. The Lancet, 373(9660), 349-351; Mayer-Foulkes, D. (2008), The Human Development Trap in Mexico. World Development, 36, (5), 775-796; Robi Kurniawan, ShunsukeManagi (2018), Measuring long-term sustainability with shared socio-economic pathways using an inclusive wealth framework, Sustainable Development, 0(0)

[9]Inglehart, R., Foa, R., Peterson, C., &Welzel, C. (2008). Development, freedom, and rising happiness: A global perspective (1981–2007). Perspectives on

psychological science, 3(4), 264-285; Boateng, R., Heeks, R., Molla, A., & Hinson, R. (2008). E-commerce and socio-economic development: conceptualizing the link. Internet Research, 18(5), 562-594.

[10]Cattivelli, R., Tirelli, V., Berardo, F., & Perini, S. (2012). Promoting appropriate behavior in daily life contexts using Functional Analytic Psychotherapy in early-adolescent children. International Journal of Behavioral Consultation and Therapy, 7(2-3), 25-32; Reichstadt, J., Sengupta, G., Depp, C. A., Palinkas, L. A., &Jeste, D. V. (2010). Older adults' perspectives on successful aging: Qualitative interviews. The American Journal of GeriatricPsychiatry, 18(7), 567-575; Proskurina, N. V., Bakanach, O. V., Tokarev, Y. A., &Karyshev, M. Y. (2015). Development of Human Potential in Countries of the European Union.

[11]Uthman, O. A., Lawoko, S., & Moradi, T. (2009). Factors associated with attitudes towards intimate partner violence against women: a comparative analysis of 17 sub-Saharan countries. BMC international health and human rights, 9(1), 14; Skevington, S. M. (2010). Qualities of life, educational level and human development: an international investigation of health. Social Psychiatry and Psychiatric Epidemiology, 45(10), 999-1009.

[12]Malouff, J. M., Schutte, N. S., &Thorsteinsson, E. B. (2014). Trait emotional intelligence and romantic relationship satisfaction: A meta-analysis. The American Journal of Family Therapy, 42(1), 53-66; S.nchez-N..ez, M. T., Fern. ndez-Berrocal, P., & Latorre, J. M. (2013). Assessment

of Emotional Intelligence in the Family: Influences Between Parents and Children on Their Own Perception and That of Others. The Family Journal, 21(1), 65-73.

[13]Mukherjee (2014). The effects of national culture and human development on environmental health, Environment Development and Sustainability 16(1)

[14]14Dube et al (2001). Childhood Abuse, Household Dysfunction, and the Risk of Attempted Suicide Throughout the Life Span. JAMA. 2001;286(24):3089-3096. doi:10.1001/jama.286.24.3089

Research Paper

Accelerating Conscious Human Development
Using the iConscious Model as an Integrative Framework
Carole Griggs, Ph.D. and Ted Strauss

Abstract

Higher stages of human development are directly correlated with increased happiness, feelings of love, reduced suffering, flow states, improved physical health, reduced mortality, and other measures of wellbeing. A new model of Conscious Human Development is offered as a means for accelerating wellbeing; both individually and collectively, internally (subjective experience) and externally (objective observations). It's theorized that applying this model using exponential technologies (such as AI) will help evolve humanity - and its environment - to thrive in an increasingly complex world.

Introduction

Human development is the study of how humans grow and mature, individually and in groups, through discernable stages. Higher stages of human development are directly correlated with reduced suffering (Szabo 2016, Klein 2011), increased feelings of love and compassion for self and others (Heffernan 2010, Homan 2016, Jennings 2009), feelings of deeper connection with self, others, and life (Pettit 2011, Pastorelli 2016) increased happiness and well-being (Bonini 2008, Welzel 2010) more continuous access to flow states (Ullen 2012, Aube 2014) improved physical health (Currie 2009, Morisaki 2014), improved mental health (Khazaei 2017, Schimmel 2009, Minas 2013), reduced mortality rates

(Singh 2012, Alvarez 2009), better outcomes as team players and collaborators (Momeni 2009, Stubbs 2008) , increased productivity (Kidwell 2011, Thirumurthy 2012), increased wealth (Susnik 2017, McKee 2009, Mayer-Foulkes, 2008, Kurniawan and Managi, 2018), improved living standards (Harttgen 2012, Th Le 2014), having more choices available (Inglehart 1981-2007, Boateng 2008), increased fulfillment of purpose and potential (Cattivelli 2012, Reichstadt 2010, Proskurina 2015), improved quality of life (Uthman 2009, Skevington 2010), more fulfilling relationships (Malouff 2014, Sanchez-Nunez, 2013), and increased concern for other species and the environment (Nukherjee, 2010). Therefore, it's evident that human development is a crucial key in making the world a better place.

Lack of development negatively impacts human endeavors and cultural wellbeing (Oesterdiekhoff 2016, Olaniyan 2012). It's also been shown that environmental constraints slow progress, and even in disastrous conditions, begin to reverse human development (Hughes, B.B., 2011).

Humanity is facing an unprecedented series of challenges, both at the level of individuals and at the level of groups, societies, and nations (Hanjra 2010, Filho 2018, Biggs 2011). The more developed people are, the wiser their choices (Oesterdiekhoff 2014). Because technology may be the single biggest factor accelerating people's impact on each other (Mukherjee 2012), we theorize that humanity can improve its own well being by applying exponential technologies, such as AI, to accelerate human development.

People living in undeveloped stages use only a tiny fraction of their potential (Oesterdiekhoff 2015, Commons, M.

L. 2008). In our view, each person's level of development directly impacts everything they do; including the technology they create. We've noticed a trend that the more developed people are, the more capacity they have for cooperatively solving increasingly difficult issues. So, as we see it, individuals and groups evolve, technology evolves, and the world evolves.

How to accelerate human development?

To accelerate human development, we must understand its primary dimensions. From reviewing prominent researchers in the field of human development (listed in Figure 1 below), we see three major dimensions as primary factors in understanding and affecting the evolution of human potential. We call these factors Development, Domains, and Views.

By Development we mean growth toward embodiment of full potential; individually and collectively. Within the Development dimension, we see three major phases, listed below. Each of the three phases includes a number of distinct stages. We describe the 3 phases as follows:

- Dual: Life and self are experienced as partial, fractured, confining, and disconnected
- Unified: All Domains are known as whole, unified, and integrated
- Singular: Dissolution of subject/object perspective

Domains is our term for the five major aspects or layers of human experience that we find are key elements of human potential. These include:

- Consciousness: The layer that is universal and registers experience,
- Uniqueness: Personality, gender, likes, dislikes, and any aspects of humans that can be assigned to "type" categories,
- Emotions: Energetic feeling-sensations such as joy, anger, fear, sadness, etc.,
- Mind: Thoughts, beliefs, and perspective-taking capacities, and
- Body: Growth of presence in and ownership of the body.

It's our theory that neglecting to consider all five of the above Domains results in slowed and imbalanced Development. When the above 5 Domains are considered throughout the spectrum of Development, some of the mysteries of human development that have previously been inscrutable yield to understanding. One example is how there have been supposed highly enlightened leaders found to cause great harm to so many people (Archer, R 2018). The addition of the Domains dimension makes clear that such people may be more developed in one Domain (ie, Consciousness), while simultaneously being quite less developed (and possibly even traumatized) in another (ie, Emotions).

The lack of integration in Development between Domains is common today in a way that may be difficult to see without understanding all five Domains. Our model shows how Development moves toward increasing levels of integration. Therefore, one aspect of understanding Development is to understand the degree of integration. We think this will be true of individuals as well as groups and societies.

Views refers to the following four perspectives that are always present; one or more can be taken at any given time:

- Subjective - an individual person's interior experience
- Observable - Anything that can be measured or perceived about an individual from the outside, including behaviors and biometric measurements
- Relational - Shared interior experience in relationships and groups, including cultural ideas and feelings.
- Systemic - Observable systems View, including economies, transportation and physical infrastructure.

Problem: Partial perspectives within human development

Over history, human developers including researchers and theorists tended to focus on partial aspects within the larger field of human development (see Figure 1). For example, most seem to study one of the five Domains individually (such as Consciousness or Emotions), or in pairs, such as psychosomatic (Mind and Body), or psychological (Mind and Emotions). Within Views, most tend to focus on one or two of the four Views, such as correlating subjective experience with objective behavior, such as brain wave patterns or other biometrics. And many mix one or two Domains with one or two Views over a partial range of the Development we can see.

Figure 1 shows how specific developers cover various and often partial aspects of Domains, Views, and Development. To see the most updated charts we produced that separately show 1) developers by extend of maturity through our 3 Phases, and 2) developers by Views within Domains, please visit: https://iconscious.global/research-charts/.

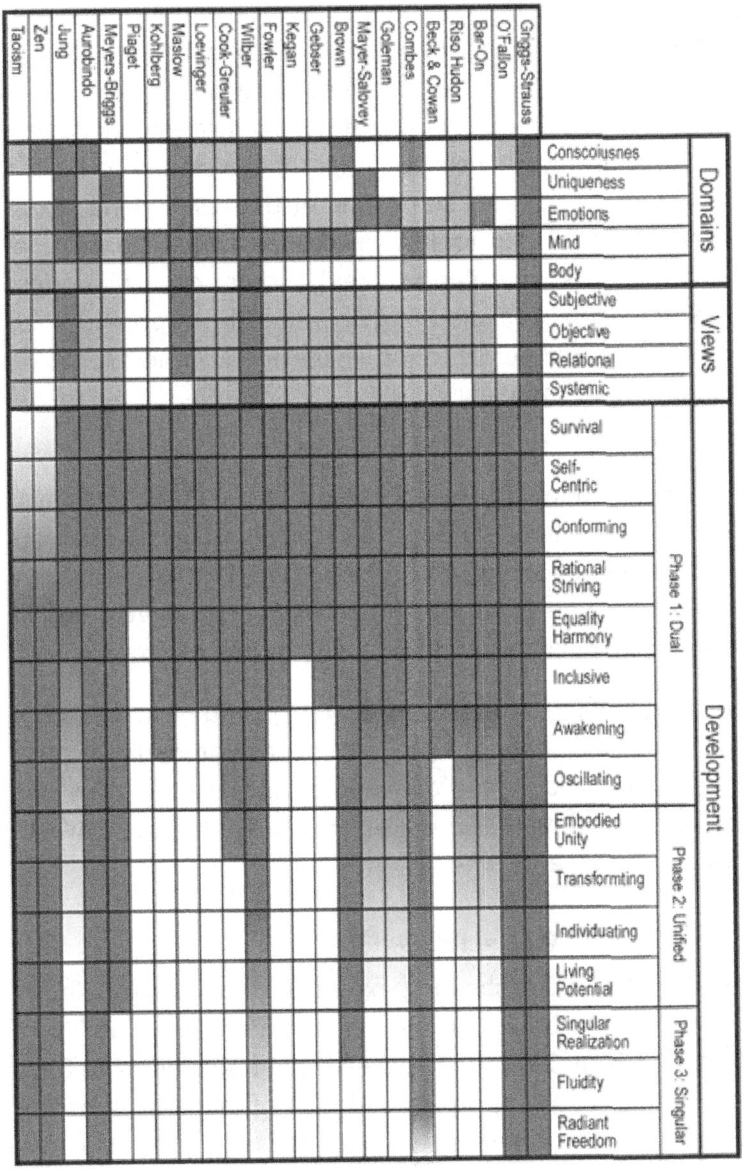

Columns (top labels): Taoism, Zen, Jung, Aurobindo, Meyers-Briggs, Piaget, Kohlberg, Maslow, Loevinger, Cook-Greuter, Wilber, Fowler, Kegan, Gebser, Brown, Mayer-Salovey, Goleman, Combes, Beck & Cowan, Riso Hudon, Bar-On, O'Fallon, Griggs-Strauss

Row groups:

Domains
- Consciousnes
- Uniqueness
- Emotions
- Mind
- Body

Views
- Subjective
- Objective
- Relational
- Systemic

Development

Phase 1: Dual
- Survival
- Self-Centric
- Conforming
- Rational Striving
- Equality Harmony
- Inclusive
- Awakening
- Oscillating

Phase 2: Unified
- Embodied Unity
- Transformting
- Individuating
- Living Potential

Phase 3: Singular
- Singular Realization
- Fluidity
- Radiant Freedom

Figure 1

In Figure 1, the dark boxes indicate focused study or teaching by the developer, and the lighter boxes indicate that this area has been touched on but not deeply studied or elucidated. An empty box means we found no significant work in that particular Domain, View, or Stage of Development by the developer. As you can see, some of the researchers in the above chart focus primarily on one particular Domain, ie: Consciousness (Aurobindo, Zen), some on Uniqueness (Ruso/Hudson, Meyers-Briggs), and others primarily on Mind (Cook-Greuter, O'Fallon, Piaget), etc. Others focus on one or two of the Views.

Each of the above developers/theorists has their own way of naming and defining development and each have their own set of criteria for defining the extent of stages. Some call them stages or levels, and some define that by describing expanding spheres of meaning making, ego-development, values, perspective taking, or ability to process complexity.

The field we're working in is very often split between consciousness evolution and human development. Because these fields that are often studied in separate silos, we coined the phrase "Conscious Human Development" to bring them together.

Problems with partial perspectives

The Figure 1 chart showing extent of development clearly shows that the bulk of study done to date falls within Phase 1 (Dual) of our 3 Phases of development. According to Beck and Cohen (2006), approximately .1% of the population are developed beyond what we refer to as Stage 7. Because there are so few living stably in more developed Stages, it has been extremely difficult to discern enough observables that together would define a stage that might be measured with reasonable statistical significance. This in turn, makes it hard to gather subjects for testing, which continues the mysteries of what constitutes more advanced stages of development.

The Sentence Completion Test (SCT; developed by Loevinger and elaborated by Cook-Grueter, 1999) is a good example of this problem. It was developed using people who, in our model, are in Stages 3-6. It therefore cannot identify stages beyond that. This underscores the problem that there is little data available about development beyond Stage 7 in our model.

The appearance that previous developmentalists have unknowingly conflated various dimensions of development into a single linear description also causes tremendous problems when it comes to understanding nuances of development. In our experience, if the five Domains aren't considered separately, lack of integration cannot be seen. For example, if someone is well developed in Consciousness, but poorly developed in Emotions, any model that conflates these dimensions cannot show which of these aspects are more or less developed.

We find that the lack of an understandable, comprehensive, integrated perspective causes a number of major problems for researchers and theorists. We've organized the problems according to the 4 Views in our model as follows:

1. Subjective: In our experience, most people don't fully understand how humans holistically grow and evolve,

which in turn causes significant confusion, stuckness, slowed development, depression, and hopelessness about fulfilling one's own potential.

2. Objective: Lacking a comprehensive framework, developers haven't known how to integrate objective data with subjective, relational, and systemic data.

3. Relational: Lacking a holistic model of relational development causes difficulty understanding how the many relational development systems are related to each other and to the other major dimensions of human potential.

4. Systemic: Lack of an integrative model makes it hard to vision how to design systems to support humanity's most direct thriving.

It's not that we feel all developers should include everything all the time. Actually, we find it's imperative that developers and researchers focus on small areas in order to go deep. We're pointing out that what's needed for a holistic understanding of the depth and breadth of human development is a model that shows how all these aspects integrate and interrelate. This suggests a powerful need for a comprehensive, holistic model that brings together all major dimensions of human potential, and shows the relationships between the parts. While most developers have focused on partial areas, the need for an integrated perspective is getting stronger as humanity's need to evolve to survive its current challenges is getting more urgent.

Solutions

While much work has been done to divide the realm of human development study into its many aspects (per above), little work as been done to create a single, comprehensive, and accessible model that reveals how important dimensions of human potential integrate and affect each other as we grow and mature. In our opinion, such a model, especially as it becomes increasingly scientifically validated, would have enormous positive impacts on the quality of life for all humans, both individually and collectively.

Other developers and models have made huge contributions to the field of human development in one or more aspects within Development, Domains, and Views. However, until Ken Wilber's AQAL model (Wilber, 2005), almost none have shown how all these aspects integrate with each other, as you'll see outlined in Figure 2.

In theory, we agree Wilber's scheme encompasses all possible ways of studying the evolution of human potential. In practice, we find that most are challenged by the attempt to visualize and realistically apply these five dimensions to their life and/or work. As a result, it seems a small percent fully understand it or can use it to make predictions, conduct tests, or create practical applications.

To accelerate conscious human development, we therefore undertook the task of modeling it in a way that is integrative, easy to understand, comprehensive, accessible, and with high resolution. To accomplish this, we have:

a. Integrated 3 major dimensions of human evolution: Development (stages of growth), Domains (Consciousness, Design, Emotion, Mind, and Body), and Views (Subjective, Objective, Relational, and Systemic). In our experience, integration is the heart of acceleration. If development is lagging in any particular Domain or View, it slows evolution in all other Domains, and creates imbalances that will impact integrity and the experience of wholeness.

b. Combined decades of experience helping thousands of students to evolve in integrated ways along with our study and background knowledge of 100+ systems and models of consciousness and human development.

c. Detailed how growth occurs in each Domain, enabling us to offer specific practices we have found to be most effective for each Domain in every Stage.

d. Consolidated what dozens of developers have found from - hundreds of studies - for Stages 1-6 (pre-transpersonal).

e. Expanded the resolution especially in the upper Phases between Stages 7-15 which are either non-existent for some researchers work, or vague in others, using others' theories and our experience working with thousands of students and clients over decades.

f. Clarified the full extent of conscious human development we can currently see so others can see the territory, avoid common detours, and progress more directly.

g. Included Ken Wilber's Quadrants, renaming them as our 4 Views

h. Clarified 3 Phases of Development; based on 3 fundamentally different orientations to self, others, and life.

i. Added average descriptions for each Stage of Development in each Domain, so users can see what integration looks like.

j. Developed an assessment which reveals growth edges

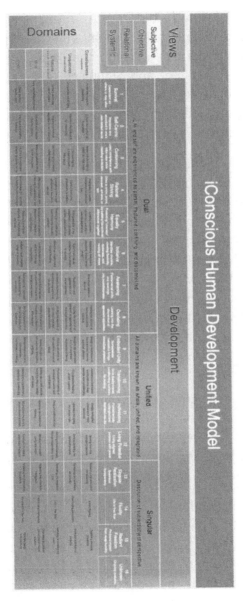

Figure 2

The model shows the three primary dimensions: Development (horizontally), Domains (vertically), and Views (in the top left corner). Development is broken into three Phases (Dual, Unified, and Singular), and each Phase is further broken into stages. To make it easy to understand how a user can find developmentally appropriate guidance, we highlight their growth edges in yellow.

To insure the model is comprehensive and can include, for example, information about States and Views within all Domains and stages, we also needed to be able to expand the data within each Field without limit. Additionally, we wanted that data to be easy to search and easy to apply to individuals who seek targeted information and resources. To achieve that, when a user clicks on any Field (cell) in Layer 1, it brings up Layer 2 within that Field, (bottom). Layer 2 allows for the endless addition of data, searchable by Views, states, or any other criteria.

Future directions

We see two main directions for further evolution: 1) further research, validation, and evolution of the iConscious model, and 2) applications for individual and collective transformative technologies (online and otherwise).

There are currently four primary ways we plan to continue evolving this model: 1) research the accuracy of Field definitions, 2) expand the Development dimension as more people evolve and Stage 16 becomes more clear, 3) further define the needs of each Field, and 4) expand the Field resources. And lastly, the more users interact with the model, the more the most effective practices will rise to the top.

We see the iConscious model eventually being used in a wide range of technologies involving humans, because helping humans evolve impacts all human endeavors, and through humans, and all life on Earth. We are involved in developing applications using conversational agents, screen avatars, and robots, and we expect to see other developmental models used in many platforms as they become available, including in human enhancement technologies designed to overcome the limitations of the body. We also see data generated with developmental models being used in business, governments, education, and all organizations as a framework for individual, systems, and content development. Even VR, AR, and gaming will benefit from embedding developmental frameworks.

References

Alvarez, J. L., Gil, R., Hernández, V., & Gil, A. (2009). Factors associated with maternal mortality in Sub-Saharan Africa: an ecological study. BMC public health, 9(1), 462.

Archer, R (2018) , An Examination of Ethics and spiritual teaching, retrieved from https://www.scienceandnonduality.com/an-examination-of-ethics-and-spiritual-teaching/

Aubé, C., Brunelle, E., & Rousseau, V. (2014). Flow experience and team performance: The role of team goal commitment and information exchange. Motivation and Emotion, 38(1), 120-130.

Beck, D., Cowan, C. Spiral Dynamics: mastering values, leadership, and change. Blackwell Publishing, 2006.

Biggs, D. (2011), Are we entering an era of concatenated global crises? Ecology and Society 16(2): 27.

Boateng, R., Heeks, R., Molla, A., & Hinson, R. (2008). E-commerce and socio-economic development: conceptualizing the link. Internet

Research, 18(5), 562-594.

Bonini, A. N. (2008). Cross-national variation in individual life satisfaction: Effects of national wealth, human development, and environmental conditions. Social indicators research, 87(2), 223-236.

Cattivelli, R., Tirelli, V., Berardo, F., & Perini, S. (2012). Promoting appropriate behavior in daily life contexts using Functional Analytic Psychotherapy in early-adolescent children. International Journal of Behavioral Consultation and Therapy, 7(2-3), 25-32.

Cook-Greuter, S. Postautonomous Ego Development: A Study of Its Nature and Measurement. Integral Publishers, 1999.

Commons, M. L. and Goodheart, E. A. (2008). Cultural progress is the result of developmental level of support, World Futures, (64), 406–415

Currie, J. (2009). Healthy, wealthy, and wise: Socioeconomic status, poor health in childhood, and human capital development. Journal of Economic Literature, 47(1), 87-122.

Filho, W.L (2018). Using the sustainable development goals towards a better understanding of sustainability challenges, International Journal of Sustainable Development & World Ecology.

Franzen, A., & Meyer, R. (2010). Environmental Attitudes in Cross-National Perspective: A Multilevel Analysis of the ISSP 1993 and 2000. European Sociological Review, 26(2), 219-234.

Hanjra, M.A. (2010). Global water crisis and future food security in an era of climate change, Elsevier, Food Policy (35) 365–377

Harris, A., ul Islam, S., Qadir, J., & Khan, U. A. Persuasive Technology for Human Development: Review and Case Study.

Harttgen, K., & Klasen, S. (2012). A Household-Based Human Development Index. World Development, 40(5), 878-899.

Heffernan, M., Quinn Griffin, M. T., McNulty, S. R., & Fitzpatrick, J. J. (2010). Self-compassion and emotional intelligence in nurses. International journal of nursing practice, 16(4), 366-373.

Homan, K. J. (2016). Self-compassion and psychological well-being in older adults. Journal of Adult Development, 23(2), 111-119.

Hughes, B.B. (2011). Forecasting the Impacts of Environmental Constraints on Human Development, Human Development Reports Research Paper

Inglehart, R., Foa, R., Peterson, C., & Welzel, C. (2008). Development, freedom, and rising happiness: A global perspective (1981–2007). Perspectives on psychological science, 3(4), 264-285.

Jennings, P. A., & Greenberg, M. T. (2009). The Prosocial Classroom: Teacher Social and Emotional Competence in Relation to Student and Classroom Outcomes. Review of Educational Research, 79(1), 491-525.

Khazaei, S., Armanmehr, V., Nematollahi, S., Rezaeian, S., & Khazaei, S. (2017). Suicide rate in relation to the Human Development Index and other health related factors: A global ecological study from 91 countries. Journal of Epidemiology and Global Health, 7(2), 131-134.

Kidwell, B., Hardesty, D. M., Murtha, B. R., & Sheng, S. (2011). Emotional intelligence in marketing exchanges. .Journal of Marketing, 75(1), 78-95.

Klein, S. (2011). The availability of neighborhood early care and education resources and the maltreatment of young children. Child maltreatment, 16(4), 300-311.

Robi Kurniawan, Shunsuke Managi (2018), Measuring long-term sustainability with shared socioeconomic pathways using an inclusive wealth framework, Sustainable Development, 0(0)

McKee, M., Suhrcke, M., Nolte, E., Lessof, S., Figueras, J., Duran, A., & Menabde, N. (2009). Health systems, health, and wealth: a European perspective. The Lancet, 373(9660), 349-351.

Malouff, J. M., Schutte, N. S., & Thorsteinsson, E. B. (2014). Trait emotional intelligence and romantic relationship satisfaction: A meta-analysis.

The American Journal of Family Therapy, 42(1), 53-66.

Mayer-Foulkes, D. (2008), The Human Development Trap in Mexico. World Development, 36, (5), 775-796

Minas, H. (2013). Human Security, Complexity, and Mental Health System Development. Global Mental Health: Principles and Practice, 48.

Momeni, N. (2009). The relation between managers' emotional intelligence and the organizational climate they create. Public Personnel Management, 38(2), 35-48.

Morisaki, N., Togoobaatar, G., Vogel, J., Souza, J., Rowland Hogue, C., Jayaratne, K., . . . Network, N. H. R. (2014). Risk factors for spontaneous and provider-initiated preterm delivery in high and low Human Development Index countries: a secondary analysis of the W orld H ealth O rganization Multicountry Survey on Maternal and Newborn Health. BJOG: An International Journal of Obstetrics & Gynaecology, 121, 101-109.

Mukherjee, S., Chakraborty, D. (2012). Is there any Relationship between Environment, Human Development, Political and Governance Regimes? Evidences from a Cross-Country Analysis. Munich Personal RePEc Archive MPRA Paper No. 19968

Oesterdiekhoff (2014). Psychological Stage Development and Societal Evolution. A Completely New Foundation to the Interrelationship between Psychology and Sociology, International Journal of Philosophy of Culture and Axiology 11(1)/2014

Oesterdiekhoff (2015). Interrelations between the brain, psychological stage development, and societal evolution, Anthropological Notebooks.

Oesterdiekhoff, 2016. The origins of the world wars I and II and the contribution of the cognitive-developmental approach to the explanation of the 20th century's catastrophe, Russian Journey of Sociology (3) 20-34

Olaniyan, A. and Aladegbola, A. I. (2012). The Political Economy of the

New Slave Trade in Africa, Global Journal of Human Social Science, (12), 14

Paloniemi, R., & Vainio, A. (2011). Why do young people participate in environmental political action? Environmental Values, 20(3), 397-416.

Pastorelli, C., Lansford, J. E., Luengo Kanacri, B. P., Malone, P. S., Di Giunta, L., Bacchini, D., . . . Bornstein, M. H. (2016). Positive parenting and children's prosocial behavior in eight countries. Journal of child Psychology and Psychiatry, 57(7), 824-834.

Pettit, G. S., Erath, S. A., Lansford, J. E., Dodge, K. A., & Bates, J. E. (2011). Dimensions of social capital and life adjustment in the transition to early adulthood. International Journal of Behavioral Development, 35(6), 482-489.Proskurina, N. V., Bakanach, O. V., Tokarev, Y. A., & Karyshev, M. Y. (2015). Development of Human Potential in Countries of the European Union.

Reichstadt, J., Sengupta, G., Depp, C. A., Palinkas, L. A., & Jeste, D. V. (2010). Older adults' perspectives on successful aging: Qualitative interviews. The American Journal of Geriatric Psychiatry, 18(7), 567-575.

Sánchez-Núñez, M. T., Fernández-Berrocal, P., & Latorre, J. M. (2013). Assessment of Emotional Intelligence in the Family:Influences Between Parents and Children on Their Own Perception and That of Others. The Family Journal, 21(1), 65-73

Schimmel, J. (2009). Development as happiness: The subjective perception of happiness and UNDP's analysis of poverty, wealth and development. Journal of Happiness Studies, 10(1), 93-111.

Singh, G. K., Azuine, R. E., & Siahpush, M. (2012). Global inequalities in cervical cancer incidence and mortality are linked to deprivation, low socioeconomic status, and human development. International Journal of MCH and AIDS, 1(1), 17.

Skevington, S. M. (2010). Qualities of life, educational level and human development: an international investigation of health. Social Psychiatry and Psychiatric Epidemiology, 45(10), 999-1009.

Stubbs Koman, E., & Wolff, S. B. (2008). Emotional intelligence competencies in the team and team leader: A multi-level examination of the impact of emotional intelligence on team performance. Journal of Management Development, 27(1), 55-75.

Sušnik, J., & van der Zaag, P. (2017). Correlation and causation between the UN Human Development Index and national and personal wealth and resource exploitation. Economic Research-Ekonomska Istraživanja, 30(1), 1705-1723.

Szabo, S. (2016). Urbanisation and food insecurity risks: Assessing the role of human development. Oxford Development Studies, 44(1), 28-48.

Thirumurthy, H., Galárraga, O., Larson, B., & Rosen, S. (2012). HIV treatment produces economic returns through increased work and education, and warrants continued US support. Health Affairs, 31(7), 1470-1477.

Thu Le, H., & Booth, A. L. (2014). Inequality in Vietnamese urban–rural living standards, 1993–2006. Review of Income and Wealth, 60(4), 862-886.

Ullén, F., de Manzano, Ö., Almeida, R., Magnusson, P. K., Pedersen, N. L., Nakamura, J., . . . Madison, G. (2012). Proneness for psychological flow in everyday life: Associations with personality and intelligence. Personality and Individual Differences, 52(2), 167-172.

Uthman, O. A., Lawoko, S., & Moradi, T. (2009). Factors associated with attitudes towards intimate partner violence against women: a comparative analysis of 17 sub-Saharan countries. BMC international health and human rights, 9(1), 14.

Welzel, C., & Inglehart, R. (2010). Agency, values, and well-being: A human development model. Social indicators research, 97(1), 43-63.

Wilber, Ken (2005) AQAL model, retrieved from http://integralrelationship.com/aqal-high-rez/

Made in the USA
Middletown, DE
03 November 2022

14002877R00156